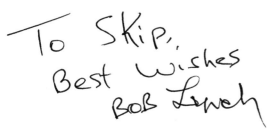

D0867505

A Letter Marked Free

A Powerful and Gripping Account of a Combat Soldier in WWII

Robert Lynch

About the Title

The book's title refers to a U.S. government ruling during WWII that mail sent home by U.S. military personnel was at no cost. In lieu of a stamp the word "FREE" was to appear in the upper right corner of the envelope. Thus was born *A Letter Marked Free*.

First published by Dog Ear Publishing
4010 W. 86th Street, Ste H
Indianapolis, IN 46268
www.dogearpublishing.net

dog ear
PUBLISHING

ISBN: 978-160844-419-9

This book is printed on acid-free paper.

Printed in the United States of America

Dedication

This book is dedicated to the many voices of FREEDOM.
May they always be heard, never grow dim,
and forever be remembered.

AND

To all guardian angels who, with irrevocable love,
watch over, guide, and protect us on our journey through life.

Private First Class Robert C. Lynch

Only the soldier really lives the war. The journalist does not. War happens inside a man and that is why, in a certain sense, you and your sons from the war will be forever strangers. If, by the miracle of art and genius, in later years two or three among them can open their hearts and the right words come, then perhaps we shall all know a little of what it was like, and we shall know then that all the present speakers and writers hardly touched the story.

—Eric Sevareid, journalist

Acknowledgments and Sources

Everyone is familiar with the meaning of the letters TLC (tender loving care). We all need a daily dose of TLC. Your doctor does not have to write a prescription for this vital medicine. It is yours for "free."

However, just as important to me was an ingredient called "encouragement." Mix TLC and encouragement on a day-to-day basis and you have a happy individual. My wife Roberta, children Kathleen, Robert Jr, Brian, and Christopher, and grandchildren supplied my needed daily requirements. I am forever indebted to them.

Someone had to be responsible for typing my manuscript. The initial typing was done by my granddaughter Caitlin Moynihan. The job of translating my scribbling and deciphering my thoughts, as well as typing changes and corrections, was undertaken by my daughter-in-law, Sue S. Lynch of Atlanta, Georgia. Their contributions were invaluable. I am extremely grateful to them.

Ms. Kay Feely Ladd took care of my correspondence with the French governmental agencies and the mayor of Vesoul, and assisted in preparing the war photographs.

A major problem arose when a decision was reached to locate WWII pictures. Major Crystal Oliver, Army Public Affairs, Washington, DC, threw me a life preserver and assumed full command. She contacted various governmental and 3rd Infantry Division entities, explained my situation, and requested their assistance on my behalf. Their response was instantaneous! The matter of obtaining war photographs was quickly resolved. I owe a debt of gratitude to the major. Thank you.

Major Crystal Oliver also introduced me to Dieter Stenger, curator of Military History Museums Division, Collections Branch in Washington, DC, who steered me in the right direction for U.S. Army photographs. In addition, the major contacted Mr. Walter W. Meeks III, curator of Fort Stewart Museum, on my behalf. The results were outstanding. The curator introduced me to his special history projects officer, Sasha McBrayer. She supplied me with an extraordinary number of copies of war photos. The Society of the 3rd Infantry Division supplied the picture of the plaque in Vesoul. All these people were of immense assistance to me. I can never thank them enough.

Finally, I am forever grateful to my war buddy, friend, and hero, Russell S. Law, for his invaluable recollections and suggestions for my writings; to my wife for her continued and constant encouragement; to Brian Lynch, my son, for his faith in me and my ability to complete my writings; and to my daughter, Kathleen, and son-in-law, Tim Moynihan, who shared responsibility in finding a publisher and coordinating my efforts with them.

My primary information source was the *History of the Third Infantry Division* in WWII, edited by Donald G. Taggart. Additional war information was secured from pamphlets "Restricted—The Record," "A Brief History of the U.S. 15th Infantry from 1813–1945," and "Battle Record of the 3rd Infantry Division."

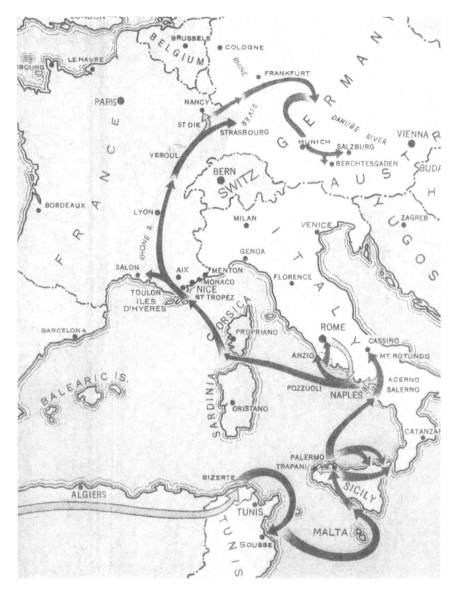

3rd Infantry Division's WWII European Theater Route

Table of Contents

Introduction

In the early morning of December 7, 1941 our nation was transformed forever when the first wave of Japanese planes struck Pearl Harbor without warning. Caught by complete surprise, most of our ground aircraft were quickly destroyed and our naval ships severely damaged. President Franklin D. Roosevelt informed the stunned nation that it was a date to go down "in infamy."

My tiny world, and the world of every American, was totally shattered by this act of aggression. The Japanese conflict, as well as the European conflict which had broken out in September of 1939, quickly developed into a worldwide massive struggle for survival. No continent, country, state, city, or individual was spared. Isolation disappeared from the face of the earth forever.

I was nineteen years old residing with my parents in Rye, New York, when the strike on Pearl Harbor took place. My close friends and I recognized that it would not be too long before every one of us would be shedding our civilian attire for a uniform supplied by the United States government. Our dreams of the future had to be re-evaluated; each of us had to decide what route to take: enlist or sweat out the draft. Without any prior discussion with my parents, I decided to enlist and volunteered for army duty through ROTC at New York University. Most of my classmates accepted the draft. As I look back I probably should have had at least a cursory conversation with my folks before enlisting, since my mother's brother, Charles L. Armstrong, had been in World War I. Unfortunately, while training at Camp Travers, South Carolina, he developed pneumonia and died on December 28, 1918.

During my early days in the army I was extremely envious of my friends living a life of relative leisure at home while I was being exposed to the rigors of basic training and preparing for combat. However, in my heart I knew my decision to enlist was the right one; there were no regrets, only a little envy. I believed strongly that tyranny could never be tolerated; it had to be obliterated. Besides, I was invincible!

From the time of my induction into the army until my discharge on November 19, 1945, I felt my family and friends did not fully understand the intense hardships a combat infantryman had to endure. Whenever I could, I would scribble a few thoughts, feelings, and words of encouragement to them so they would not worry too much about me. My folks, brother, friends, and relatives did likewise to me. Unbeknownst to me until my return to civilian life, my mother retained all my letters. These are recaptured on the following pages. A list of players (my correspondents) is located in the appendix. It should be borne in mind that all of my communications were censored. I had to be extremely careful not to disclose the name of my unit or our location. Many of my envelopes bore the stamp "Passed by (signed), Army Examiner."

In addition, my parents and friends could not send through the post office a care package (cookies, candy, gifts, etc.) without my written authorization. Consequently, many of my letters home included a "please send cookies" official confirmation which I have deleted from the letters that follow.

My letters, which I share with you, have been condensed and blended together with official army records as they relate to various 3rd Infantry Division campaigns in Europe. They vividly recount life in boot camp; the emotions of battle that I experienced as a combat infantryman under intense enemy fire; the ultimate experience of climbing into amphibious boats for a first-wave assault on Anzio, Italy, and St. Tropez, France; the full meaning of comradeship; walking with death; saying goodbye to one's friends; and most importantly: the need to pray. To those who had loved ones in the service, these letters will give you a better understanding of the sacrifices they made in the name of freedom.

CHAPTER 1

Indoctrination

The dawn of a new life burst upon me at 2:03 p.m. on April 24, 1943 when our iron horse chugged out of Penn Station in New York City and rumbled over fifty-five miles (taking two hours and twelve minutes) to Patchogue, New York. There we boarded our bus for a fifty-mile jaunt to Camp Upton, New York, which was an army processing camp.

Our problems commenced as soon as our band of brothers hit camp. There was no one available to officially sign us in. We had to wait and then wait some more for the soldier on duty to open up. Finally, we were officially welcomed on behalf of the U.S. government. A meal and a quick so-called medical exam followed. It wasn't until 8:15 p.m. that someone at the camp decided a search should be undertaken to locate bunks for all of us.

At first none could be found. However, while waiting we had a mock air raid and had to run into the woods. One recruit became scared and passed out. We finally received some blankets and an open-air tent. I slept in my clothes that night and froze. Bedtime was 1:30 a.m. As for lodgings, the draftees were the lucky ones in that they were assigned the barracks and the enlisted men awarded tents. Those in tents froze the first night; so the next evening we built a fire in the tent. Unfortunately, the soldier who engineered the construction of our fire shed fell over the stove and badly burnt his hand. He had to be transported to the first-aid station. His claim to fame spread throughout the camp—a "war" casualty on the very first day.

I never discovered whether he was awarded the Purple Heart.

Act One, Scene Two

April 1943

It felt like my eyes had just closed when I heard the reveille call. The clock showed 5 a.m.; that must be wrong, it couldn't be 5 a.m. already.

"Chow Time!" Saturday's breakfast consisted of cereal, potatoes, an orange, eggs, milk, coffee, and bread. No complaints here. A physical followed.

Three fellows passed out at the blood test. At 10:30 a.m. we went for uniforms but there were none to be located. Rather than waste time we had a quick march until 11:15 when lunch (soup, potatoes, meat, vegetables, bread) was served.

The scenario for the afternoon did not vary to any great degree other than we had three intelligence tests in lieu of an afternoon stroll through the park. Dinner at 4:15 was followed by a march until 6:30. The Articles of War were read to us. By the time we had digested the contents it was 8:30, and we were free for the remainder of the evening.

Career Path

I qualified for officers' training school. Surprisingly, I also qualified for a mechanics job, perhaps in the Air Corps. In the mechanic's test I received 122; tops was 160, but no one came close to achieving that grade. Not an awful lot got above 135.

I was surprised by my score because in civilian life I was far from being mechanically inclined. I had two left thumbs, nothing more.

I think the Army is swell. The food on the whole is fine. Even the uniform fits perfect. There is a rumor that early this week we'll be moving.
Love to All

I was afraid from day one that my career path was infantry all the way. I tried to think of some good points. That was a tough question. All I could think of was that, as compared to a job in civilian life, there were neither annual performance reviews in the infantry nor any termination or transfer requests accepted. Once you were in the infantry you were in for good. No loss-of-job worries, no human resources department to lodge your complaints with; in fact, there was no one available to listen to your complaints.

It's Off to Work We Go

April 1943

Dear Folks,

Monday 7 p.m.—Today, so far, has been our easiest day. We didn't finish breakfast until 7:30 a.m. even though they got us up two hours earlier. After breakfast we assembled and were divided into various work groups. Sixteen fellows came with me. First, we had to sweep the roads where our tents were pitched. This only took 45 minutes. Next, we were sent to get pickaxes to dig some ground. After working (or so they call it) for half an hour, several men were sent to relieve me. The remainder of the morning I just stood around and watched. At 10:45 we were dismissed and returned to wash up.

When lunch was over we gathered in the bullpen for announcements. A few of us who were to be reimbursed for the trip to Upton (actual train expense $1.90) were marched off. At the office of reimbursement we were told to come back tomorrow at 7:30 a.m. Consequently, we were free for the rest of the afternoon and evening.

Since I've been here, there has only been one day (Sunday) in which we have NOT had beans. Who says they don't feed you pork 'n' beans? We have also had pork twice. Unfortunately the food is always cold. Miss you all.

P.S. Average day is 5 a.m. to 11 p.m.

Army Benefits

Sunday—After lunch we went to pick up our "free" uniforms. The style and colors were all identical; no choices!

  2 winter underwear
  2 summer underwear
  1 overcoat
  1 jacket
  1 fatigue suit
  3 summer socks (pair)
  2 winter socks (pair)
  2 pairs of big shoes
  1 raincoat
  1 canteen
  1 food plate with knife, fork, and spoon
  1 Book of Regulations
  4 hats, including 1 helmet
  2 towels
  1 shaving kit, soap, comb
  1 tie and 1 belt

All of the above attire was thrown in one's barracks bag, and we were

marched out to receive our "free" shots. We had small pox, tetanus, and typhoid. Right after the injections everyone's arm became very stiff. Notwithstanding, we had to shoulder our 90-pound packs and tramp back to our tents with only one arm. At 2:15 p.m. we were dismissed.

In today's environment, salary and health benefits rank number one and number two in job consideration. The military takes an entirely different outlook. Without any hope of discussion, I was advised that the government would

take $6.50 a month out of my pay to cover my $10,000 insurance policy and $18.75 for a bond-a-month. That leaves me with $25.

End of discussion. Oh yes, clothing, food, lodging, and medical expenses incurred while on active duty were "free." Thank goodness for small favors. Later in my career I discovered lodgings usually were open air foxholes or bunkers constructed by me without running water, electricity, bedding, bathroom facilities, or entertainment centers. Food became cold C or K rations.

Work Detail

Tuesday 8:45 p.m.—What a day I put in and what a night I expect! We worked hard all day and ate garbage for dinner.

Right after breakfast we met in the bullpen and were assigned duties. Twenty-five of us were marched back to our tent area and given farm tools. They stuck a pick in my hand and told me to dig in. I sweated in the hot sun from 8 to 11.

I was all set for a quiet afternoon when the corporal assembled us into groups. I was picked for the work detail again and shipped off to the warehouse. My first job was to fill two boxcars full of wood. After loading the troop trains, we were dispatched to chop wood. The axes were dull and the wood unbending. I chopped for 2 hours and then some.

My pals call me a farmer. They think I look just like one in my gray fatigue suit, with my shirt tails hanging out.

Tonight is a formal inspection of our beds. Everything must be in perfect order or we'll get KP. Speaking of KP, my name is on the list for tomorrow at 3 a.m. Miss you all.

Kitchen Patrol (KP)

May 1943

Wednesday they woke me at 2:45 in the morning. About 50 of us marched over to the mess hall and were assigned various kitchen tasks. I had to wash silverware for some 4,000 men. There isn't enough silverware to go around, so you have to keep washing it over and over. By night I had dishpan hands and was dead tired. Lady Luck has forsaken me. Thursday I received KP once again. There was one saving grace. I had everything I wanted to eat, not like yesterday when we worked another mess hall and got nothing.

That evening I was almost positive I would be transferring to my permanent basic training camp; my bunk-mate made it and I did not.

It's cold and rainy. Many are getting sick. Disease is very common at Upton. I feel fine.

The food is dwindling in size. We don't get a big portion anymore. This should be my last KP duty at Upton. A new era beckons.

Friday 9 p.m.—I'm dead to the world. I've had KP Wednesday and Thursday. In the past 3 days I've only had 3 hours of sleep a night. Say hello to all.

"Sleepy Head" Bob

CHAPTER 2

Basic Training

Thirteen Weeks to Go

It's hard to believe it took two long days by train to reach Camp Wheeler, Macon, Georgia, from Camp Upton, NY. The coach was seven hours behind schedule when we finally pulled into our destination. The camp was located on twenty-four acres outside the city of Macon. For two weeks I was quarantined to the regimental area and could not leave the premises. Once the restriction was removed, I could visit Macon on Saturday nights and Sunday. In general, we were free to roam about after 6:30 p.m. any night of the week.

May 10, 1943

Lights out in the barracks is at 9 p.m. During your so-called free time (two and a half hours), you have to shine your shoes, shave, take a shower and clean your rifle. That takes more time than you have available; at night when all is finished you can sit out on a tiny fire escape and write letters by the brightness of the porch light.

There are 36 recruits sleeping in the second story of our barracks. Some of the men cannot speak English and quite a few are unable to write. I have to write home for at least 6 of them. The ages of these men range from 18 to 36. A large percentage of them are extremely overweight. More than half of the men are illiterate; most never passed the 8th grade. Those who have reading and/or writing problems have to attend class four times a week for 2 hours at a stretch. The classes last 12 weeks.

It's terribly monotonous doing the same thing day after day, night after night. To relieve the tension many recruits stay up until the wee hours of the morning playing cards. This practice is frowned upon by the commandant's office. If one is caught they could lose 2/3 of a month's pay and be thrown in the guardhouse for a month.

Our battalion is a crack heavy weapons military machine. We are considered infantry but specialize in machine gun and mortars. We study the 30mm and 50mm machine gun. Less emphasis is placed upon the rifle.

Every morning from 8:30 to 9:15 we have sitting up exercises followed by fast running, which practically kills most recruits. A few have passed out. The rest of the day is spent attending classes and marching, and marching, and marching. We have a fixed schedule to follow. Every hour a new subject is presented.

Additional equipment was issued during the first week: rifle, gas mask, bayonet, entrenching tools, and cartridge belt. On Friday we go on our first march with full pack and rifle.

Laundry is $1.50 per month, haircuts are 30 cents, candy is 5 cents and ice cream is 10 cents. Movies can be seen for the price of 15 cents. While at Camp Wheeler they will give us 13 injections for fighting in hot, tropical, areas (South Pacific, I hear you calling).

Seven miles from Camp Wheeler is the city of Macon, whose time belt is one hour different. We'll leave camp at 7:30 p.m. Saturday and arrive in good ole Macon at 6:30 p.m. What a crazy system.

As part of our training we have to see the picture *Desert Victory*.

Monday, I peeled a huge bin of potatoes while working KP for 18 hours. You can visualize me doing this work. Whenever you attend a movie and see the movie star sitting and peeling the spuds, just substitute the movie star for me. I'm learning new things every day. Cutting carrots, peeling potatoes and washing dishes are my specialties. Keeping a cold stove going is another of my jobs.

Let's Take a Hike

May 1943

Friday—The sergeant awoke us at 5:30 a.m. and gave everyone the good news. We had to take a hike on the hottest day of the year into the wilds of Georgia. It was "loads" of fun—45 pounds in fact. Our packs and rifles were strapped to our backs. As the day rolled on the packs seemed to get heavier with each step. The sweat was rolling off before we even started.

We marched for an hour and then rested 10 minutes. The dust was unbearable! It clogged your nose and made breathing exceedingly difficult. Finally, after only four miles (it seemed like ten miles) we reached camp. Our pup tents were set up, water ditches to carry off the rain were dug around the tents, and these peanut-sized tents were camouflaged. After lunch we deployed in battle formations and had mock battles. The heat kept rising all the time and by 3:30 p.m. we felt we were dying.

A weary bunch of men staggered back to home base that night. Quite a few dropped along the way. Some drank water when they returned and passed out. The hospital car took them away. To make the evening complete we had to clean and scrub the barracks.

The following day we had a gas drill. After a few moments we removed our masks and felt the effect as the gas burnt our eyes. Later we had slight whiffs of mustard and Lewisite gas. These gasses hurt one's nostrils and made others quite sick. Several received skin infections.

Measles has broken out, and as a result quarantine has been extended 2 more weeks. It's so bad we are unable to leave the barracks at night.

Saturday we were shown 2 documentary war movies on events leading up to World War II. The movies depicted the September 1931 invasion of Manchuria by Japan, the invasion and slaughter of innocent natives in Ethiopia, and Japan's invasion of China. After the showing it was announced that there were 6 more of these war documentaries to be presented at a later date, starting with the destruction of Pearl Harbor.

Marches and Rifle Range

May–June 1943

Thursday and Friday—The rain continued to come down in torrents. There was no let up. Nor was there any let up in our marching orders. We nearly froze to death in our wet clothes. When a rest break was finally called, the men fell exhausted on the wet ground. The rain water drenched us but no one cared. Saturday morning I had no dry clothes to wear. Consequently, I, along with the other recruits, had to put on wet, muddy fatigue suits. They felt lousy!

Sunday I received the local paper you sent. It was great to read the sports page again. I never know what the Brooklyn Dodgers are doing anymore. Keep sending the baseball standings. Incidentally, the cookies you mailed were not even broken. They tasted awfully good. Thanks.

Monday and Tuesday we had our initial rifle practice. My first job at the range was in the target pits pulling down, marking, and raising the targets. Tuesday I shot for record. After every shot the targets are brought down in the pit and marked. They are immediately sent up; a big metal disk is placed over the bullet hole for a few minutes. The rifleman sees the marker and records his shot in his record book, after which the disk is removed and the riflemen fire again.

Tuesday Bob Hope visited Wheeler. He did his show and then came out after the broadcast was completed and entertained us for another hour. Actually, the best part followed the broadcast.

We had chicken stew. It's the first time I've had chicken since leaving Rye. Naturally, the chicken in the stew was extremely hard to find. You really had to search for pieces!

Love,
Bob

Machine Gun

As I approached the midway mark in my basic training, I commenced training on the machine gun.

June 1943

I was on the range all day. In the morning I qualified as a machine gunner. Anyone getting above 140 is a marksman. My 156 isn't too bad. Upon completion of our target practice I had to load the guns on the trucks until 6 p.m. It seems the regular men assigned to the area get off at 5:30. No one was left except a few of us. Naturally, I was one.

Friday—Today I had to report to the firing range and shoot for record on the machine gun. I received a bad break in that my machine gun decided to turn balky. I was getting a great score and nearing the end of the drill when the gun started doing tricks. In my last round I received only 8 points out of a possible 40. That ruined me for good. My final official score was 138. (140 needed to make the grade.)

Sunday—I forgot to tell you. Friday on the range I had an "alibi gun" which means the gun continually breaks down and sprays the target instead of zipping the bullets straight in. My gun did just this, and so that is why I missed qualifying by 2 points.

The machine gun weighs 92 pounds, with the tripod weighing 51 pounds, the receiver weighing 33 1/2 pounds and the water in the gun another 7 1/2 pounds. You can shoot 400–500 shots a minute with this great little gun. The only trouble is that at that speed the barrel eventually gets too hot and is rendered useless. The average number of bullets per minute is 125. Think of it, 125 bullets in 60 seconds!

In the movies they show the actors firing the gun from the hip. That's impossible; it would rip your guts out. We have to know what each part does in the overall operation of the gun; the names of the parts must also be at our finger tips.

Mines

June 1943

During the week we learned how to defuse tank mines. According to the army, once you spot a mine, you lay on your stomach, loosen the ground and probe the area with your bayonet. This is done to locate booby traps. If you hear or hit something near the mine then you know it's a booby trap. Instead of lifting the mine right out, you disconnect the booby trap from the mine and take them both out. Sounds simple doesn't it! Friday we had a march and studied laying mine fields until eleven that evening, . . .

The above operating procedure was never fully utilized in my combat days as an infantryman. However, I did have one occasion in Italy to meet a mine face to face.

Compass

June 1943

Thursday, we were in the field the entire day. In the afternoon we marched to a camping area, ate supper, and sat around until dark. Compasses and directions were handed out. We could not show a light to read the compass unless it was covered by a raincoat.

Our route went through swamps and lowlands. It was horrible to try to find your way to our destination. At times we were in mud and water up to our knees. We climbed over rotten logs and hacked down heavy, thick vines. Luckily, we did not run into any snakes, although other squads did. The trees were old and rotten. The worst of it all was the mosquitoes that kept nipping and biting. Three soldiers were reported M.I.A. and we had to search for them. Finally, at midnight we located the missing soldiers and returned to our barracks. Coffee and cake were served.

Bayonet and Mortar

Monday—Bayonet practice is one of the toughest drills we undertake. Two squads face each other 50 paces apart. You place your rifle on the ground, run to the center, do shadow boxing, rush back and grab your rifle. The lieutenant gives a signal, and you double-time back and forth, screaming and yelling at the top of your voice all the time. Long thrust, short thrust, short jab. The army claims they simulate actual combat conditions by making us run so much. The sun steals your breath; the intense 100 degree heat only causes you to tire sooner.

Tuesday we will be studying the mortar. Each platoon fires 24 rounds; a live projectile costs $9.35. However, on the range we were advised that dummy shells would be utilized. This keeps the cost down, and the recruits alive.

Typical Menu

Breakfast: scrambled eggs, coffee, orange, one slice of bacon, and cereal at times

Lunch: Potatoes, ice water, bread, pork 'n' beans

Supper: bread, ice tea or water, stew, and some type of vegetable

We are always kicking about the meals. The kitchen never seems to have enough food. Ten fellows sit down at a table with the food already in dishes spread out before them. Someone yells "rest" and you dig in. If you sit too far away from the dishes you don't get very much. In the event you are close to the food, you might get a smell as well as a real taste.

Did I tell you that we get mashed potatoes every lunch? They give you plenty; enough to fill your fork twice.

Punishment

Monday—The bad news has been published.

Our quarters failed inspection. As punishment we have to "rise 'n' shine" at 5 a.m. every day for a week. (I can manage the "rise" portion but fail miserably when it comes to "shining" at 5 in the morning.)

Friday is scrub night. How we hate this job! You get on your hands and knees and scrub the floors with a brush. Then the floors are rinsed with hot, clean water and mopped clean. It takes nearly 2 valuable hours away from our free time.

Miscellaneous

June 1943

Tuesday night—I was scheduled to visit the dentist. At 6:30 p.m. I assembled and took the bus to the dentist's office. Unfortunately, I've lost a few teeth so far; another one is in the wings. One soldier has lost 7 to date. The dentist's motto is "pull, not drill."

The heat is still near 100. Our clothes are wet from morning until night. Once you are exposed to the sun you are lost. Your shoes begin to burn and the sweat pours off you. At night it's just as bad; you cannot sleep in this heat.

Saturday—We dug slit trenches against air attack. I made my work ten times as hard by forgetting my darn entrenching tool. Consequently, I had to dig with my bayonet and use my canteen cup as a shovel. You can imagine what fun that was for me! When I got back to the barracks the mud was caked on my body. Even after a thorough scrubbing, the good ole Georgia clay loved me so much it wouldn't let go. "I'm yours," it kept repeating.

The barracks were sprayed today to kill all those cute bugs. I must say that the bugs are so numerous they play hide 'n' seek with us. We hide while they seek us.

There is a new rule that has been posted today. Henceforth, we must wash our fatigues every night. What a mad house that regulation will create with 64 soldiers trying to wash in one basin! That will only take away more of our precious free time. The army certainly doesn't want you to be alone. They do their best to keep you moving.

I was lucky to miss guard duty Saturday night. Everyone but 7 fellows had to pull watch for 2 hours during the night. To make matters worse, once or twice it rained briefly.

The good old chiggers must be losing their touch. Their last attack was relatively mild. The itchiness is slowly but surely leaving. I scrub myself with a floor brush every night. It hurts like the devil and really rips your skin, but it helps in the long run so I don't mind it too much. Next week we again venture into the fields to play with the bugs. (Chiggers are tiny bugs that burrow into your skin and cause irritation.)

China's First Lady was in Macon this past weekend. It was certainly an important day for the citizens of Macon. We didn't receive time off to hear her speech, but it was rebroadcast several times during the day.

I'll be waking up early Sunday, July 11th. I am going to try the air waves again and call you. Sometimes it takes 6 or 7 hours to get through while at other times it's only an hour. I expect to contact the operator at 6:30 a.m. but when my call reaches Rye is anyone's guess. Jot down a few things to say so that we won't waste any valuable time. It's only 3 short minutes.

Friday we slither along the ground on our bellies while live machine gun bullets fly overhead. The corporals fire 17 inches above our heads. I'm sure no one will jump up to look around.

Recently, we tossed live grenades. This was really something! You pull the safety pin and toss. The fuse burns out in 5 seconds and off she goes! Our leaders keep impressing on us not to drop the grenade or chuck it too close. If you drop it, well, you need not worry.

New Programs, Extensions, and Furlough

June–July 1943

As of July 4th the army basic training program has been extended from 13 to 14 weeks. We do not know whether our groups will have the original 13 weeks or the new 14-week program. I understand our last 2 1/2 weeks are devoted to maneuvers followed by a 5-day leave.

I learned some more dirty hand-to-hand fighting tricks. We can snap a man's head in a second. (If you can grab it.)

Monday—Today we were told that we would be getting a 7-day furlough, not including traveling time. All that we talk about these days is the furlough. Everyone is so happy that they'll be home in six weeks. Some are chartering planes for $57 one-way. The army will charter a train for you. It is only $24 round trip.

This past week we were introduced to our new commander, Major General Brown. On June 21st, his initial review of camp procedure brought about some changes. Heat exhaustion had taken the lives of a few boys. General Brown decided there was no reason to be so tough on us; no more double-time, no more heavy packs unless on overnight hikes and no more obstacle course. . . . On Sunday these orders were revoked.

Air Alert Drill

July 1943

This will be another sleepless week. We are having an alert in camp and have to sleep in fatigue clothes with our shoes and leggings on. We will be called out sometime around 2 a.m., instructed to put on our heavy packs and forced to double-time to the next battalion. From there we will be stacked into trucks and taken to our posts. I will get behind my trusty 50-caliber machine gun and be prepared to fire at enemy planes. No planes will be seen, but it will be good practice, or so they say. When I return there will be no use going to sleep. Yep, that's right, I have KP all day. Twice in the last 4 days! How lucky can one get?

I think the food here is being rationed. It's getting worse and worse. For supper less than 3/4 of the men bother going to the mess hall. I generally go over to the PX for milk and a frank.

Infiltration Course

July 1943

Our group seldom remains in Wheeler anymore. It seems that we are in the field 2, 3, or 4 times a week. Next week we are away from camp every day except Monday and Saturday.

Friday, our company had the intense pleasure of negotiating the infiltration course. We started on a 5-mile march inland to an extremely wooded area. A portion of the woods had been cleared; there were trenches at both ends of this hundred-yard "football field." At the sound of a whistle, all recruits scrambled out of the trenches and started forward into the face of live machine gun fire. We had to crawl with our rifles and bayonets over logs and under barbwire and at the same time watch out for dynamite traps. The ground was sandy but soaking wet from a recent rainstorm. Some soldiers froze from fear and couldn't negotiate the course.

Bivouac

July 1943

I am in the bivouac area and writing everyone using the back of my mess kit for support. Those ever-loving bugs are so thick I can hardly see what I am scribbling. They are into everything, especially me! My legs are a mass of ugly scabs and red bumps.

The temperature was approaching 100 degrees as we reached the machine gun demonstration area. Once there, we stripped. Off went our packs; off went the gas masks. We lay in the shade 10 short minutes and sipped water ever so slowly. Moments later, we were on our shaky feet and into the brilliant sun for 2 1/2 hours of instruction. The water just rolled off my back; my fatigues began to stink. All were so tired we couldn't sit still to watch the demonstration. As the temperature rose, we got hotter and hotter and cursed more and more.

After an eternity in the sun, we put our packs on and started for the bivouac area. By the time we arrived no one had any water. However, a water bag was set up so that we were able to refill our canteens.

Immediately, we took off our packs, unrolled them, and set up house. Once the tent was up, my buddy and I squatted down and ate an orange, candy bar, and your cookies which I had brought along in my mess kit so they wouldn't break. For supper I ate a hard-as-nails biscuit and some cookies. The corn beef was too salty to eat. It wasn't long before I called it a day and trudged back to my cave-man's tent to finish up your cookies.

Did I tell you that some crook swiped $32 from our platoon? Men are losing things left and right (mostly on the right though). Our platoon is restricted until the money is returned; everyone has been searched. The results were far from fruitful.

The Tuesday night bivouac was called off, but not before running into a multitude of problems. We left camp at 8 o'clock with heavy packs (full gear) and gas masks. The sun was down but the temperature wasn't!

Our Company A marched for 2 hours before finding the bivouac area. Once we took the wrong trail and had to retrace our steps. It goes without saying—there wasn't a dry scrap of clothing on my body by the time we reached the tent area.

In the pitch darkness we set up tents, entrenched them, and lay down completely exhausted. The officers let us rest for three-quarters of an hour. Suddenly, without warning we were told to break camp. It started to blow and blow. Inside a few minutes all hell broke loose. Rain came down in torrents! We put on raincoats, but the water only rolled off our coats and soaked us. Inside a few minutes our shoes were also floating. (Now I know what "walking on water" means.) Waves of water rushed down the roads; we had to tramp through the mud and newly created rivers. Once in a while someone would fall or slip. He'd be lucky not to drown.

At one in the morning we spotted our home base camp and increased our cadence. The mess hall was open, and some recruits were there to feed us doughnuts, and, guess what, WATER! It felt wonderful to get our dirty, wet fatigues off. Even the snacks tasted great.

Wednesday morning we could sleep until 10:30 a.m. I awoke at 7:00 and ate a tasty breakfast of cereal, milk, and pancakes. As a reward for arising early, I got stuck for a policing detail. At nine I commenced to clean my rusty rifle. What a mess! Rust and water were in the barrel. I scrubbed for almost an hour before success came my way.

I am taking a few cookies with me on our afternoon hike. We will sleep under the stars (or should I say, rain clouds). Thursday night we'll be back in camp just in time to scrub the floors.

On Friday I was room orderly. I stayed around the barracks all day, swept the floor, washed the latrine and kept the hot water furnace going. I didn't have to run the obstacle course with the boys. There was another accident though. A soldier from the first platoon fell from the 35-foot wall. He turned over in mid-air and landed with a thud on his back. His hand hit the ground first; thereby breaking both his hand and fall.

This heat hasn't let up, but you are probably mighty hot in New York. I hate to think of August. I don't see how it could get any hotter!

A Call Home

July 1943

Dear Willie,

Early Sunday morning: I am sitting waiting for the telephone company to get my call through to Rye, so while I am doing nothing, I thought I would write. This week we shot the .30 caliber light machine gun. It's a small gun that weighs almost nothing. The papers say that the marines shoot this gun from their hips at the Japs. The gun, however, is air-cooled and so the barrel gets extremely hot. The marines must have burnt their hands trying to shoot it. We also fired the rifle grenade. You shoot the projectile from your ordinary rifle. A little contraption fits on the end holding the grenade. You pull the trigger on the rifle and away it flies. The grenade explosive is a tightly kept military secret. No one knows what it is made of, except they claim it does wonders when fired at tanks. (Someone is daydreaming, I think.)

Sunday—10:30 a.m.: It was wonderful to hear everyone. Didn't those 3 minutes pass fast? The operator had no trouble after she reached Washington. Once past there she sailed right into NY. I could hear the operator going north. She reached White Plains next to last. My heart jumped when she said Macon calling, and you said "hello." They held me up while I deposited the coins. It's 55 cents a minute. Before leaving Wheeler I'll call again.

It only took two hours to reach you. That was a good break. If I called at noon I would have to wait 6–7 hours for a call to New York.

Not many fellows bother calling because they sleep late on Sunday and haven't time to wait all day. I am used to getting up at the crack of dawn! So the call for me was easy.

The lieutenants still claim they don't know whether our basic training will be 13 weeks or 14 weeks and include a nine-day bivouac. It would appear that to date all the Wheeler boys are eventually shipped to the West Coast and off to fight the Japs.

Driving Class

July 1943

Dear Folks,

Monday was a real easy day. We either sat down all day or drove trucks. Camp Wheeler is trying to teach the entire company the art of driving these big trucks. We rode back and forth over the highway, taking turns driving. I drove a one-ton truck. It has 5 shifts instead of the usual 4 for cars. Whenever you start to shift you <u>must</u> double clutch, otherwise the gears will grind. All of us have to complete 32 hours of driving, finalized by an obstacle course test. Another bivouac is looming in the horizon with a night march mixed in. Heavy packs and gas masks are included. We will be required to pass another test, this time on mechanized attack. Besides the usual marching, we will spend time in bayonet drill, hand-to-hand combat and close order drill. Fortunately, the temperature has dropped to the mid 90s. However, the rain never seems to miss Macon, Georgia.

A new mandate has just been issued. Henceforth, soldiers must write their name, the word "free," followed by one's serial number (12114106), on all mail envelopes.

Tenth Week

July 1943

Dear Folks,

So meat is scarce in Rye? I don't think we are much better off. Beef is not known in Georgia, only pork and fat. I see by the paper there is also a shortage of eggs up north. Does that affect you? The price of fruit seems high here. I got upset at the fruit man when he tried to charge me 35 cents for a dozen Florida oranges. Several months ago I used to buy them for much less.

The camp is full of rumors. Some sound good. We just completed our 10th week in basic, with 4 more to go. That's right, our basic training has an extra week tacked on. Fourteen is our lucky number.

Drove a truck for the final time. I qualified for a government license which is good in any state.

Endurance Test

July 1943

Everyone is really dead tired this evening. Our endurance test was tough! The heat has skyrocketed upward. In one company of 200 men some 50 recruits passed out in <u>one</u> afternoon; two of these men never snapped out of it.

Thursday morn we rose at four o'clock and ate a hearty breakfast; by 5:30 a.m. we were on the road with heavy packs, gas masks, and rifles. We hiked to a new area and started our warm-up exercises. The first cute exercise was a mere 33 pushups; second on the list was a 300-yard dash, followed by a horse and rider race for 200 yards. The third brilliant move was a race where you ran, crept, crawled, and jumped. Finally, we did a slap-happy exercise of diving all around on the ground. At that point in time we were deemed ready for the nut house, ooops, I mean our march.

We started jogging and ended running double-time. Every time someone started to fall out we had to take his pack so he could continue with us. I finished carrying 2 gas masks, 2 rifles, my pack and myself. My legs felt like water when we reached our barracks. Several boys had to be carried in by the other guys, but everyone was credited with having made it. No one was left behind.

After the march we took the remainder of the morning off. All were too tired to do anything but lay on their bunks and try to get a little rest.

In the afternoon we went to the bayonet course for an hour. We were just too tired to do anything. When the day was finally over we went straight to bed. Unfortunately, it was too hot to sleep. However, by 10:30 p.m. my eyes closed for the night.

Attack and Conquer

July 1943

The weeks are getting tougher. This coming week we have to run with mortars, dig fox holes in the blazing sun, dig mortar emplacements and have a 20-mile march. We don't have to wear leggings anymore. The brass have stopped that for good. Last Saturday we sat around in the barracks, listened to the "Hit Parade," and ate all the cookies I had left. What a feed! No one has any money left.

Friday we attacked and conquered a make-believe enemy village. The enemy shot rockets over our heads, fired machine guns and automatic rifles down the streets, and discharged dynamite in our vicinity. We are just invincible.

The first man would rush the nearest building, toss a grenade inside the building, and fall flat on his face on the ground. After the grenade went off (5 seconds after pulling the pin), the soldier would rise up on all fours. Number two man would run, jump on number one's back, and vault through the window. After he had captured all the men inside the building and had searched the rooms, he would call out "all clear" and the others would enter. Once inside we would take up firing positions, covering the men on the other side of the street. As soon as all men had entered the building across the street, we would rush out and do the same thing on the next building. This was done all the way down the street. On two-story buildings we had to enter from the second story. Grenades were tossed into both the first and second stories. Incidentally, the grenades were only made of flour, but live ammunition was fired at us, well over our heads, as we approached the buildings. We fired at dummy targets on the side of the houses. (I got hit once.) In addition we were instructed to keep yelling at the top of our voices as we ran into the various stores, trying to frighten anyone who might be inside.

I cannot ever recall this attack and conquer concept being used in actual combat.

The End Is Near?

July 31, 1943

I don't know where to begin. One thing is certain and that is we will never forget July 31st, 1943. On this Saturday morning they told us our 5-day furlough passes had come through, and we would soon be going home. Boy were we a happy bunch! The sun smiled down on us in all its glory. As an added attraction we were informed that after our leave, a boat ride would be awaiting most of us. To me that sounded swell. Hopefully, it will be Europe. I am emotionally ready and itching for combat.

In the afternoon our clothing was checked. We had to display every bit of clothing we owned. Once this inspection was completed we packed everything away. During the check-up the camp radio broadcast great news—"no ten-day bivouac." What a great break! Now the chiggers won't be able to slice me to pieces.

An hour later a wild, slap-happy group of soldiers formed for their final inspection. The lieutenant called the company to attention. It was then that the ax fell. We were to have a 17-week training cycle. Seventeen weeks! We'll be here in Wheeler the hottest months in the summer! Now I have to "look forward" to the next five weeks. You will never finish checking off how many weeks I have left. I guess you will have to read my letters for the next five or more weeks.

I have enclosed a paper clipping from our Spoke paper. Another new basic training exercise is to be added to our program. As you can see, in the landings in Sicily and the ensuing battles the number of casualties (killed) were quite heavy. However, the army did learn a valuable lesson. Of the total killed, more than 10% died while landing from the barges—in other words they drowned because they couldn't swim to shore with their heavy packs and rifles strapped to their backs. This is an astonishing figure! Henceforth, all training camps must teach swimming if they have the facilities. In our added weeks we have to learn to swim with our clothing, packs, and rifle. (Why packs and rifles I don't know.)

We were paid Saturday and just about everyone in our battalion went to town. The report emanating from headquarters was the place (Macon) was full of "drunken soldiers." Today, Sunday, many are throwing away their money via the dice.

Saturday morning we had a free-for-all. All our dirty fighting was put into use. You had an opponent, and it was up to you to throw him to the ground and pin him there. If you threw your man you still stayed in the ring and fought someone else. I tossed three easy guys before losing. It was a lot of fun anyway. Tops was one fellow pinning four men.

New Schedule, Four Weeks to Go

August 1, 1943

The army is a screwy place! I never saw anything like it. This Monday evening we were to have a night problem, but, as usual, in the afternoon it was cancelled. We returned to the barracks to sleep instead of playing all night. You don't know whether you are coming or going. (Study this last word to get the true meaning.)

All day we toyed with mortars. We would double-time with them, set them up, sight the target, play we were dropping in shells, dismantle the mortars, and do the whole exercise over again. This is what I would call an interesting and exciting day. On top of this we had to dig slit trenches after setting up the mortars. Fortunately the only enemy was the sun.

How is the castle in Rye looking? Does daddy cut the hedges, push the lawn mower, rake the grass, clip the hedges and water the garden every night? He does? Atta boy!

Cookies came today from Macy's. They were lovely chocolate chip cookies. Only one thing was wrong—there were 6 or 7 ants to each cookie. What a mess! Hundreds of ants digging in.

The meals they serve us in the field are swell. Lunch Tuesday had potatoes, roast beef, and lemonade in addition to the cookies/ants. Is your mouth watering? Well, close it because this evening we ended up with beans and spaghetti.

I am the number one customer for nail polish in our company. I just bought a carload of nail polish for our coming bivouac. I recognize the chiggers will attack me, but I'm going to kill them immediately thanks to the nail polish.

Boys Will Be Boys

August 1943

For the past few days (Thursday and Friday) we have been digging, digging, and digging. Anyway, we had to build mortar and machine gun emplacements in addition to our regular foxholes. I scouted around the area and found some ground that was easy to work with a shovel. Once completed I lay down and fell asleep. Luckily, no officer was around. (They were probably asleep too.) I must have slept 2 or 3 hours. Suddenly, I awoke with water falling on my face. It was a thunderstorm and did it come down in torrents.

Eventually we ate supper, pitched tents, and built fires to dry our clothes by hanging them over a line stretched across the bonfire. We lay on our blankets around the crackling fire, sang songs and tossed the bull well into the night.

The following morning we were routed out at 5:30 a.m. After breakfast our camp was dismantled, and for the rest of the morning we carted guns around, dug foxholes, and threw mud bombs at one another when the lieutenants weren't looking. I'm sure you never thought I'd revert to my childhood and play with mud pies in the army. I goldbricked most of the day and only dug about 24 shovelfuls all day.

It was terribly hot; in fact the commanding officer thought it was too hot for us. He had us remake our heavy packs (blanket, raincoat, and shelter half) into light packs (raincoat). Even though our packs were lightened, many fell out on our march back to camp.

We now have beans six times a week. Went to see Bing Crosby in *Dixie.* Incidentally, on the road to Macon there is a drive-in theater. *This Is the Army* is playing around town.

One of our boys died this past week. While on the infiltration course he got hit by a ricochet bullet. He didn't have his dog-tags on and so the medics couldn't find his blood type until it was too late. Henceforth, we must at all times wear dog tags.

Mock Battle

August 1943

Lately, we have been doing plenty of digging. Saturday we had a mock battle. One platoon occupied the emplacements we had dug; the rest of us had to attack them. My platoon had to wade through dense swamps to reach the left flank. Once in the swamp you would sink halfway up your legs. Regardless of all the work it was fun.

The attack began at 1:25 p.m. At the allotted minute we rushed out of the swamp with bayonets fixed. Running uphill was without any concealment. As a result we had to rush for 10 yards, hit the ground, roll over, remain quiet for several seconds, and then rush forward again. When we were about 100 yards from the top, we ran forward, yelling at the top of our voices at the enemy. I still can't quite understand what good it will do to yell in English at the Germans or Japs, but our leaders insist on doing it. It is awfully tiresome to keep these tactics up so long.

Wednesday noon in the middle of our machine gun drill we received a major shock. Names of 40 soldiers were read out, and they were told to report back to camp. By Thursday evening they were packed and had received new equipment. Their train comes to camp on Saturday to pick them up and deposit them in Camp Meade, Maryland.

Our 17-day bivouac starts this coming Monday. We are in the field for 3 days, return for 1 day, and leave Wheeler again for 2 weeks in the field.

Ring worms are very numerous in our barracks. Several lads are completely covered with them. Are they terrible! Just about 4 fellows haven't had heat rash. Some have had it for 10 long weeks. I happen to be one of the lucky ones—no heat rash.

By today's paper (Friday) things look great in Sicily. They had better hurry up and invade Italy.

Saturday night was a madhouse. Beds were turned over and clothes tied into knots. What a mess! Most of the guys returned drunk as a skunk. You can't blame us. We'll be in the field 2 1/2 weeks.

Pre-Bivouac Days

August 1943

Maneuvers start on Monday. How we dread this! We will be in the field for 17 straight days. Upon returning our cycle will be over and there will be nothing left to do except scrub the barracks again and again. Your cookies arrived today, thank goodness. They will come in handy the next 2 1/2 weeks. Don't send anymore until I find out what's in store for me in the immediate future.

A Typical Soldier's Evening After Retreat

August 1943

Let me give you a brief description of a soldier's day upon returning to the barracks. He doesn't sink into an armchair and sip away on a lovely, cool Tom Collins. Oh no! Instead he rushes into the barracks, elbows his way upstairs, tosses his rifle on his bed and struggles to get the darn pack off his back. Occasionally, it sticks on a button and won't get loose. He'll curse wildly until another weary, sweaty soldier pal helps him. Thank goodness that d—- pack is off!

Someone screams out twenty minutes until retreat. Again there is a mad scramble to the bathroom to wash up. It's wonderful to get out of that hot, smelly room.

Yep, ten minutes to go. You take off those horrible wet fatigue clothes and put on your uniform. Ah, now you feel like a soldier.

Five minutes left, but footsteps are heard on the stairs. It is the corporal looking for eight "volunteers" to clean machine guns. A third wild rush is heard as the lads dive under the beds to escape detection, but in a loud booming voice the corporal calls out your name and off you go to clean guns. There is no justice in this army.

After a hasty retreat from the mess hall you put the finishing touches on your gun and bring it back for a checkup. As usual the sergeant finds some slight speck of sand on it; the gun is recleaned again.

Eventually, the gun is okayed and you are on your own. Anything that you want to do is at your disposal, but before going to town you merely have to wash your fatigues (and this is a bloody riot when 10 guys get in the shower at once). Someone scrubs the wrong foot or else one turns on hot water instead of cold. This sets off the fuse and in a moment the shower room is in an uproar. Anyway, you must wash your fatigue clothes, shave, take a cooling shower, polish your shoes, scrub your rifle, and write half a dozen letters. Of course lights go out at nine o'clock but that doesn't matter: it's all free time.

On occasion by some freak of nature if one manages to get everything done, then he can go to town and get some food to eat.

The average soldier must be content to forget about town and think of the wonderful time he could have had if he had been on the ball and gotten the few things he had to do done in time.

Just before closing his eyes in blessed sleep the soldier listens to a few late rumors, shrugs his shoulders, wishes he could be home, and then turns over on his side and falls into dreamland.

"Oh How I Hate to Get Up in the Morning"

August 1943

You back home probably don't know too much about a soldier's quiet, peaceful day. Anyway let me enlighten you on the beginning of "his day."

The schedule says you are to rise at six o'clock, but our motto is "don't believe everything you read." Our sergeant can't read anyway because he gets us up at 5:30 so we can be ready for reveille.

From a wonderful sleep you are rudely awakened by your dear sarge. You blink your eyes, moan a little, give a loud grunt and turn over to get a few extra seconds of shut-eye.

Eventually, you struggle to your feet, search for your pants and shoes, and then stagger down stairs to wash your face. Even the water doesn't help revive you.

Upstairs you go, cursing the sergeant and wondering why you are the only platoon that gets up early. Your bed looks like a cyclone hit it, but it was only you spending a restful night. It must be straightened out a little, and the rules say you must remove all sheets each morning and turn your mattress. Naturally you're a good soldier and know this fact, but that's as far as it goes. Instead of doing all this unnecessary work, you merely tighten the sheets a mite and call it quits. The bed is made, and that's the main thing.

While you are putting on your shirt the bugle blows and everyone rushes madly for the stairs. Those who are not as quick as you are caught in the "5:30 rush hour traffic" and are carried outside.

Half-heartedly you dress right and stand at attention as the bugler blows reveille. The sarge gives out the order in which you will eat chow and naturally your platoon is last.

Today you feel extra hungry, and so you dash to chow before the other platoons can collect their senses. They call you a chow hound, but they are only jealous.

After a wonderful breakfast of eggs (which you don't eat) and coffee, you return to the barracks to discover that today all beds must be taken out and aired. This means that you must rip off your sheets and carry the mattress outside. All that early work for nothing. Bah!

Eventually, your bed is outside and you have swept the floor clean as a whistle. There isn't a speck to be seen anywhere, but the sergeant calls it filthy and says we must scrub it down that night. Next time he'll get us up at 5, he warns.

Five minutes before falling out we find we have to police the orderly room. Volunteers are again looked for, and, of course, you are one of those lucky ones chosen for the job. Off you rush on the detail to pick up everything that doesn't grow. Since you are an average soldier, you see pieces of paper but turn the other way and longingly search the ground. "There's a match stick there," yells the sergeant, and you take ten minutes bending over to pick up the match. Who cares about a little match?

Once back at the barracks you zip upstairs, grab your canteen and cartridge belt, reach for your pack, and run downstairs with your rifle. You have no water and so have to fight your way into the washroom to fill up. Meanwhile the sergeant stands at the top of the stairs screaming madly for you to get on the road. "Last one out cleans windows tonight," he bellows. Only fools pay any attention to his threats, so you continue filling your canteen.

By 7:20 you are on the road and look around for the other platoons. To your amazement you find you are the first platoon formed.

At the command "fall in" you snap to attention, dress right, and then attempt to stand still. Out on the roadway the radio broadcasts the latest camp bulletins: "light packs today."

Naturally, you have on a heavy pack, and so again you madly fight your way upstairs to take off your heavy fields and make a light one. Sweat pours off you, but you don't mind it. You have grown to understand the army way of life by now. They do everything backwards; nothing makes sense.

At last you are ready (or so you think). It is then that you discover you have forgotten your helmet and for the fiftieth time this morning you fly upstairs and grab it.

When 7:30 rolls around you are standing in ranks panting like a mad dog. (Too bad I am not English.) The lieutenant marches up and bellows out "Right," which is immediately followed by the command "Face." You turn to the right and are ready for the 7-mile march. While waiting to move out the corporal sneaks up behind you, looks at the mangy pack on your back, and tells you to tighten it up in your next break. Bah! Always on the go.

Maneuvers

August 1943

The first day of our maneuvers is over and I am none the worse for this day. The real work begins tomorrow and ends 16 days hence.

We were routed out of our sheets on day one at the ungodly hour of 5:30. I would have loved to have had about 5 more hours of sleep, but they said <u>NO</u>!! However, I took 12 extra winks and finally fell out. I ate an inviting breakfast of cereal; forget the eggs.

Everyone returned to the barracks after that great meal and brought their sheets, barracks bag, and laundry to the supply room. Upon re-entering our home the whole contingent had to open their lockers wide and move their beds out from the wall. The place was a mess, but we eventually got it swept spic-and-span. (I'm turning into a fine housekeeper.)

Before pulling out I brought my money to the orderly room for them to hold. How much did I turn in? Well, that's a secret but if you can keep a secret I'll let you know. I had $23 in cash and that $10 money order which you sent me months ago. I figured on cashing and using it for furlough money. What a laugh!

We were ready to leave at 7:30, but somewhere things got bawled up as usual; we didn't start until 8:15.

Up, up, and up the mountain we scrambled. We reached the heavens and continued on (you might have known I couldn't stop there). Anyway, the whole battalion kept marching onward to Iverson Range. There we saw a demonstration of a mock battle. The terrain was very rough, and so there were several casualties. Live ammunition was shot at targets that popped out of the ground. One corporal had bullets land right beside him and others had the same experience. Since the course is so extremely dangerous, we recruits will not be allowed to fire live ammunition here for someone could easily be killed.

Following this demonstration we moved into our bivouac area and began to select our real estate locations. Lunch (beans, potatoes, tomatoes, bread, and pudding) was soon called and away we ran.

Following lunch we erected our tents and entrenched 'em. I must admit, we were the first to finish digging the slit trenches. I chose an area that someone else had previously dug and filled in. What a hard worker I am! Once our tents passed inspection by the zoning board (sergeant), we began to improve our surroundings.

The first thing we did was to straighten up a slope so that it formed a chair. Behind the so-called chair we erected two poles and connected them with branches. We tied the back together with green vines that I found in the woods. All that was missing was a table; so we set to work to build one. Up went various twigs and branches until a crude writing table had been made. Now our home was complete. It was just like "23 Oakwood Ave, Rye."

The entire afternoon was spent constructing our temporary residence. Before we knew it, supper was called. They fed us franks and (no, not beans this time) corn. After eating, we picked up our barracks bag and trudged on home. I fell into my chair, turned on the radio, sipped on a cold drink, and wrote letters. What a day! What an army! What a man! (You will probably contest this last word.)

Battle Stations—Initial Phase

August 1943

Time marches on. This morning we were out on the battle field carrying live ammunition. They gave each soldier 48 rounds to fire. You can imagine the noise we created when you consider every man in our platoon fired this many rounds. Add to this 2,000 rounds for the machine gun, and you have the battle picture.

The terrain was full of deep ravines, trees, and uneven slopes. By the time you stormed the top of the enemy-held hill, you were dead tired. Walking back from the range to our bivouac area was mighty difficult.

For lunch our menu showed pork and potatoes. I was starving since I skipped breakfast (eggs 'n' bread). After lunch we sat around and reviewed a lesson on gas attacks. Finally, we were sent back to camouflage our tents. I couldn't find my tent after supper; it was so well camouflaged.

The highlight of the evening was a shower in our homemade bathroom. My buddy and I heated water over a fire and ran a wash cloth over our bodies. Then we took turns dousing each other with water from our canteen cups. What a great way to bathe!

The evening was extremely busy. We had to thoroughly clean our guns since they were fired so often. After that came the usual shaving, washing of fatigues, and underwear. In the woods where our tents are set up, it gets dark very early. You spend just about all the light hours getting ready for the next day. My sleep last night was very sound. (Who am I kidding?) The ground was very uneven, so I kept twisting and turning. As a last resort I leveled the ground so my rear end wasn't higher than my head.

Wednesday night my prayers were answered. All morning it rained off and on. We sat around and slept in our tents until 10:30 a.m., after which we cleaned our rifles. My rifle is so clean I am afraid the enemy would see my reflection and gun me down. Anyway, during the morning rainy spell, I lay down and caught those 40 winks of sleep that I needed.

The afternoon was devoted to gold-bricking.

Once the rain stopped I did nothing but lay in the shade of the trees and play I was guarding machine guns. The only work I undertook was to carry a 46 lb. mortar base plate up a long hill. It was hot slavery but only took a mere 10 minutes.

School will be back in session by the time I get back to Rye. Billy ought to like going to high school. It's a great time in his life.

All Out Warfare

August 21–23, 1943

Today, we had an all-day battle. We met in the assembly area at which time reconnaissance patrols were sent to locate the enemy and find how strong they were. I was put in charge of my 4-man patrol. Out we went into the thick forests. We fought our way through dense thickets until we reached an enemy hill. An enemy patrol, meanwhile, came by and we hid until it had vanished. By creeping and crawling we reached the outer defenses. I sent a message back to company headquarters telling them the location of the enemy guns. After this, the remaining 3 of us continued along to gather more information. Unfortunately we had a skirmish with the enemy and were captured and questioned. My messenger, however, got back safely, and so the attack plans were drawn.

Naturally, other patrols were sent to gather information, but they got caught too. Just before our escape there were 12 of us in the prison compound. When the guard wasn't looking 2 of us sneaked through the wire and back to our lines.

After lunch our company was ready for the attack. We led the men to the enemy-held ground and opened fire. The other riflemen, followed by machine gunners and mortar men, came and gave us support. We continually drove the enemy back, but would lose some ground on counter-attacks. The end came at 3:15 when we charged with bayonets. The enemy broke, and the battle was over. By the time we reached camp we were plenty tired. I didn't feel like working on my rifle; it had to remain dirty.

Did I freeze last night! My feet felt like icicles when I woke during the night. I put stockings on before I could go back to sleep. I still can't understand what happened. You could actually see your breath in the early morn. My pal and I made a fire outside our tent to keep warm! What a crazy place is Georgia!

We again scrubbed one another tonight. After scrubbing floors, this is a cinch. I merely grab the guy's head, ram it in the ground, put my knee in his back and commence scrubbing. After that's over I throw boiling water on him.

Friday Night—Another day spent in battle tactics, but on top of this we hiked some 8 miles to arrive at different areas.

At first 5 fellows and I were detailed to guard the rear of our column. In case of attack, it was our job to rout the enemy while the rest of our men continued on their way. Just as we arrived at a turn in the road a machine gun cut loose with blanks. We surrounded the gun and I crept forward into position so as to fire and knock them out. Finally, I hit a good spot and, likewise, opened up. As a result the gun was put out of action, and we continued on our way. (For this aggressive action I was awarded the distinguished Wheeler Cross.)

Sometimes the enemy would fire from an empty barn, and we would give chase. If the enemy was too large for us to handle, we would call the machine gunners for assistance.

At the last station we became machine gunners. Shortly thereafter someone yelled "gas," and we had to put on our gas masks and continue moving forward. As we removed our gas masks, the whistle for air attack was blown, and we dispersed into the woods. Before some could reach the wooded area, a plane was swooping over them, dropping flour sacks. (This simulated bombs and machine gun fire.) As a defense against air attack we set up our machine gun and opened fire. The plane came back and forth about 6 times, just skimming the tree tops every time. It was only flying 125 miles an hour, but at such a low level it seemed to be really ripping.

When the attack was over we walked 3 1/2 miles back to the bivouac area and called it a day. We were plenty tired, but it had been fun, and we had learned something. (There's no place like home.)

Saturday Night—Every morning and night we build a fire to keep warm. It's wonderful laying on your blanket by the fire and just dreaming and watching all the thousands of stars twinkling at you. What a sight! I could lay under the trees and stars all night. Come to think of it, where else would I be?

Your cookies arrived today and were too grand for words. Out here you can't get any cookies, so when these came the boys really went for them. They certainly hit the spot!

The food is really good. Only for the first two days did I have any reason to yell. After that the food improved tremendously. The veal they served us was excellent, as were the franks, steak, and pork. Yes, one day we had potatoes, steak, and chocolate milk. It was a feed!

Today we had scouting problems (finding enemy positions) in the morning, and then in the afternoon we cleaned our rifles. (Something new.) It was a real easy week. Only a week and a half left of bivouac. Then we'll wash up and be leaving. (I hope!)

At night we have boxing matches between companies. In addition, Saturday they had several of our boys put on skits. Some guys could sing pretty good. Several used to play or sing for different bands, so they got together and put on a show. It wasn't bad for the short time they had to prepare. Afterwards ice cream and cake (the first time it's been in our company) were served.

A truck came out with some candy and cookies. Did that stuff disappear fast! Sunday they'll be out again. You can buy a bar of candy, a package of cookies, or cigarettes.

What do you think we got today? You'd never guess, so I'd better tell you. They gave me my new steel helmet; the one used in combat in overseas fighting. We have to get used to carrying or wearing it, and that's why everyone was issued one. I suppose I'll turn mine in before leaving, but most will keep them for their trip.

Chaos Reigns

August 24–26, 1943

We are moving today but not by any national moving company. We have to break-down our tents, fill up our slit trenches, pack our barracks bag, roll up our heavy field pack, and smother our fire pit and home-made chairs.

I washed all my clothes this Sunday morning. Hopefully, they will dry before I move out. As for my socks, I scrubbed them in my new steel helmet.

We have been having battles all week. One day we had a real airplane attack with bombs. The plane flew right over our heads and fired. One flour bomb hit a soldier's rifle and another bounced off a helmet. (No one was in it.)

Sunday night we had another screwed up attack. We left our old area at 6 p.m., marched 12 miles to our new enemy position. In this exercise we were to be the enemy and had to attack the rest of our battalion as they passed by. Everyone had a flour bag which he was to toss at the approaching soldiers. By midnight our scouts reported the column had been sighted. However, by some twist of fate, a second battalion was coming in the opposite direction which no one bothered to mention. Both battalions passed each other at the exact spot where we were laying in the bushes awaiting to attack. Anyway, out we scrambled, yelling and screaming at the top of our voices and throwing flour at all the troops. In a minute the road was in an uproar! One battalion didn't know what was happening, and they ran every which way. Our second battalion was on the lookout but could do nothing with the first battalion running through their ranks. Our screaming only confused men more. Panic set in. It took hours to reorganize the men and various battalions. Eventually, the units moved on, but not before 2 to 3 hours were wasted looking for lost men. Some of the soldiers in the "unexpected" battalion were practically frightened to death. Finally, in the wee hours of the morning we arrived, battle worn, at our bivouac area and pitched tents. Blessed sleep fell upon us.

Our next night problem was not quite as complicated as the last one. We were to infiltrate the enemy positions that we had built in the morning. In order to do so, we had to cross swamps and dense woods. We were divided into 7-man patrols, furnished with a compass, and sent on our way. For hours we trudged along, holding on to each other's rifle so as not to lose one another. We succeeded in eluding all enemy patrols and reached the enemy's command headquarters. To add realism, sound effects were broadcast simulating planes diving, bombs bursting, and machine guns firing. We crept across a large field, but as we neared the compound the enemy detected us, and we were captured. Eventually, the exercise was finished, and we marched back to camp for cookies 'n' ice cream.

The End Is Near

August 1943

I am glad Jean renewed my subscription to the Tribune for 2 weeks. I read it at night after I've completed my chores. On Sunday I catch up on the news in "This Week."

Every evening we get together and sing songs. The only song that really stands out is "South of the Border." The "Marines Hymn" is number two on our hit parade.

This is it! My furlough has come through. The train will pull in Labor Day, and I will probably arrive in New York late Tuesday night or Wednesday depending on when we exit Wheeler. I will be home for 5 days. When I leave Rye I report to Fort Meade, Maryland.

Tonight, Sunday, starts our 20-mile march. We will keep moving at night for the next 3 days. No more tents to pitch. When we do sleep, it will be on the ground, without blankets or anything. Before leaving we practiced once again with the machine gun and mortar.

See you in 5 more days!

Dear Folks,

Thursday night—Everything is over for me at Wheeler. I haven't slept more than 3 hours a night since Saturday, but that doesn't matter. I'm finished and that's what counts.

After the maneuvers were over, we obtained water to shave. We washed, shaved, ate lunch, and then marched into camp singing our heads off. A band met us at the main gate and brought us in.

The following day was clothing check. We had our equipment checked throughout the day. Some companies haven't even finished yet, and it's now 7:30 p.m. I expect new clothes in certain categories. We still don't know when we'll leave, but it is almost positive that our train will take us away from Wheeler on Monday, Labor Day. That will be a great day for me.

I'm dying to see the kittens; they must be awfully cute. Luckily, I can see them before you give them all away. See you soon. The days left are very few.

Love to All,
ME

Finale

September 1943

We turned in our gas mask, canteen, and mess kit to the supply room. On Saturday we will unload our shelter half and on Monday, Wheeler will unload little 'ole me. Hot dog!

My ticket to Meade is paid by the government; I pay from Baltimore to Rye.

Your homecoming menu letter came this evening. That meal you are preparing sounds swell, but it will be even better when I sit down and devour it. I doubt if I'll be in town before Wednesday.

Graduation

I have just graduated from basic training and received my diploma. Personally, I think I failed every subject, but the Army Brass told me I am a "superb specimen." Superb is putting it mildly. I carry around 128 pounds of bone and muscle, although don't try to have me show you my muscle. On a clear day you might be able to see a ripple if you look closely, but that is only on special occasions.

I will hate to leave Georgia; it was such a lovely place. I could never complain about not getting my just share of the sun's vitamins, in fact I had a mite more than the allotted requirement. Whenever I begged for relief, the Army advised me the sun was doing wonders for me, and I must not complain. When I started crawling in from forced marches on my hands and knees with my tongue dragging behind, I grasped the true meaning of "doing wonders for you." It's a wonder you don't drop dead.

Today the whole battalion assembled for a farewell speech by the major. He stressed Wheeler soldiers are really outstanding. (Naturally, we knew this fact.)

Ah nuts! I'm not on the Tuesday orders. Now I've got to look for Wednesday. I hope your food keeps. I might not get home much before Friday night. Tonight, Monday, I have guard duty from 10:30 to 12:30 followed by KP.

I received two new pair of shoes from the army. Nothing fancy. We checked clothing all day; putting them on and taking them off. We did the same thing in the morning and the identical thing in the afternoon. Nothing makes sense! (I guess that qualifies me as being "clothes crazy.")

Everything is topsy-turvy. Everyone is leaving this afternoon, Wednesday, except 13 guys. Unlucky thirteen! And I'm number 13 too. I will be disappearing Friday morning and will reach dear Rye late Saturday. Your cookies came this morning. We will devour them after lunch. The package was missent to Ft. Benning, Georgia. This is the second time this happened. Anyway, I have your cookies and that's the main thing. I tried to call you this morning twice, but the operator couldn't get through. This is definitely the last Wheeler letter you will get. I'll be eating Saturday supper with you. See you then!

Love to All!

Dear Folks,

I have a "book" in my pocket which states I have been granted a five-day furlough. In case you are not familiar with the Army way of doing right things the wrong way, let me explain. When I received my furlough papers, the Army printed a long list of fellows who are going on "leave." In case you get careless and lose one, the military whips up 15 to 46 similar lists for you to take along as a precaution. Your name is on every list along with Joe Twiddlebird's and Robert Snoodlepuss'. You don't care whether Bill Zilch lives in New York or Wapponackoe and Bill himself doesn't care because he knows where he lives. Nevertheless, the Army thrives on complications, and so when you leave camp you are presented with this 50-page gold-bound book. It's so bulky you don't know where to stuff it. Eventually, you get the brainstorm to buy a suitcase; you can always use a suitcase. May as well buy one now and get it over with.

Camp Wheeler Report Card

Camp Wheeler, located outside Macon, Georgia, was the first and largest infantry replacement training center in the U.S. The terrain was hilly; the sun was burning and relentless; the rain was frequent; the swamps were endless; recruits laid in mud day in and day out; the chiggers were everywhere; the chow was passable; the marches were unreal; weariness was eternal; griping was continuous; sweating never stopped; lectures were boring; guard duty/KP seemed to be never ending; mail call was the highlight of the day; battle courses were rugged; barbed wired obstacles were routine; bivouac was hard to accept; barracks were the cleanest places on earth; despair was ongoing; Sunday was the best day of the week; bathroom facilities were extremely limited; entertainment was scarce; sleep was blessed; a "life of your own" was a fantasy; cussing was a manner of speech; privacy was non-existent; and rumors were rampant.

Overall Camp Wheeler turned out topnotch infantrymen, well trained in the fundamentals of warfare. Wheeler soldiers are a credit to their country no matter what theater of operation they were assigned.

CHAPTER 3

Movin' On

Camp Meade, Maryland

September 1943

Dear Gang,

Evenin' folks, how ya'll? It was tough to return to reality after those few days in Rye. Lovely Georgia is now a thing of the past. For the next few weeks, I will be fighting the bugs at Camp Meade, Maryland. After that it will be _____. Your guess will be as good as mine.

I have a surprise for you. Henceforth, I will be getting a monthly government check for 20 bucks in addition to my bond which is sent to Rye. Today we signed our overseas statements. The salary (overseas duty) increase of 10%, we are told, will take place next month; thereby bringing my monthly take-home pay up to $23.25.

Saturday, I went to the movies and saw *Phantom of the Opera* starring Nelson Eddy and Susanna Foster. Tonight we are planning on seeing *Best Foot Forward* with Harry James. *Johnny Come Lately* with James Cagney is scheduled for next week.

The captain advised us that we would be in Maryland 2 or 3 weeks at the most. Everyone is hoping for a nice boat ride to England. How would you like to get a swell free trip like that?

[I had always thought my first cruise would be a romantic experience with exquisite cuisine, uncompromised luxury, extraordinary amenities and the finest of beds, linens and pillows. What a rude awaking befell me.]

I'll try to get home for a couple of hours some Sunday. Put the key under the mailbox and I'll let myself in. Before leaving the US I have to get my hair scalped. The barber should leave only 1/2 inch of hair on my head.

I'm still on the (un)lucky side and drawing KP. I worked in the mess hall until 9 p.m. Usually, the KPs get off duty at 7 p.m., but naturally when I'm on duty we are assigned extra duties. I got stuck cleaning the smelly grease trap.

It's back to the rifle range this week with a few marches thrown in for good luck. We fired our rifles from 6:30 a.m. to 6 p.m. The game warden pinched me for shooting out of season. You see I bagged a moose and 6 geese instead of a bull's-eye. I guess the bullets must have curved. Maybe I shouldn't have closed my eyes before firing. Anyway, Friday I fire for record. (I'm gunning for 2 deer and 8 ducks.)

I'll be glad to leave here. One week is almost over. I guess I am just restless, but I don't seem to care for Meade. At night we do nothing but sit around, write, or drop by the movies. I wish we had a radio but that's out. Signing off for tonight. This is station M E A D E, in Baltimore.

Love to All

Dear Folks,

No luck reaching Rye this weekend. Sunday we were issued all new equipment; received underwear, socks, gloves, field jacket, and gas mask. I broke my watch again. This time it really won't run. I don't think you should buy me a new one. I'll pick one up overseas.

Friday night we scrubbed the barracks after which we went to see *Watch on the Rhine*. *Sahara* is coming next week along with *Wintertime* with Sonja Henie. No passes again this weekend. I think it's almost time to bid goodbye and head out.

Love You All

This would be my last letter written from the USA for several years. As of September 30, 1943, my address would be an APO number; Europe my theater of operations; the 3rd Infantry Division my home base; death my constant companion.

"Over the Boundin' Main"

October 14, 1943

Dear Folks,

I guess I'd better turn the clock back to my quick U.S. departure. From Ft. Meade, Maryland, I was ushered on a train heading toward Patrick Henry, Virginia. My stay in Virginia lasted a mere 96 hours. It was on the night of October 4, 1943 that I boarded a train which dropped me in Newport News, next to the gang plank, of our transatlantic cruise ship (the SS Never Sink). Red Cross furnished us with hot coffee. As your name was read, you tossed your barracks bag over your shoulder and walked up the plank. (Now I can boast I walked the plank.) An Army band was there to see me off, and they kept playing as we boys marched into the future.

Right away I jumped into the hole of the ship, grabbed a bunk, and went on deck to enjoy the sights but instead got stuck for a detail; we had to load the ship with hundreds of C rations for us to devour when we land in Africa.

At 5:30 we ate chow and went on deck again. A short time later a pilot's tug drew alongside and moved us out into the main channel. As our boat slowly dug into the waves, we all stood and watched until it was too dark to see home.

It hit us hard at that moment. Call it homesickness for lack of a better word.

Note: In 1943 it would take a Liberty ship 18 days to cross the Atlantic. Victory ships made the crossing in 12 days; regular troop transports took only 10 days. Needless to say, I was awarded the pleasure of utilizing the services of a Liberty ship.

The tossing of the ship woke me next morning and I went on deck to view the sights. Land was nowhere to be seen. All that I saw were ships and water. It's just like the pictures you see in the newspapers—convoys of gray ships dotting the horizon as far as the eye could see.

After breakfast the army boys began feeling a mite strange and by noon more than 25% of the men were seasick. The ship was soon a complete mess! Luckily, I managed to escape the casualty list. It took a couple of days for most fellows to acquire their sea legs. The clean-up detail was something else.

The Army feeds us twice a day—once at eight o'clock (breakfast) and then supper at six. Around noontime I got awfully hungry but there's nothing to eat. The hardest meal to keep down is breakfast. Powdered eggs are just about uneatable because they are so salty. The other dehydrated vegetables aren't too bad, but the eggs—bah! Our food is either from cans or is dehydrated. Gourmet it's not.

Our sleeping quarters are extremely tight. Everyone sleeps in the ship's hole. The distance between you and the man above is the distance from your elbow to your finger tips. So help me that's all the breathing space we have. It's really a tight squeeze!

I have the whole day to myself. Generally, I go on deck to read or write. I've done more reading this past week than all my previous college years.

On the 2nd day out the Red Cross came through again. They distributed to every soldier a carton of cigarettes (all popular makes), a candy bar, and a special package containing writing paper, envelopes, soap and container, razor blades, shoe laces, sewing kit, shoe shine rag, 25 cent pocketbook (I received *How to Think*), playing cards, and matches. That certainly was extremely thoughtful of them. My grab bag gifts came from the Red Cross Nassau County chapter, Mineola, NY.

Dice games consume most of our daylight hours. Some guys have won hundreds but most have lost their pants (I still have mine).

I must wear my life preserver at all times on deck and must have it nearby after dark. Incidentally, the ship is completely blacked out every night.

I read *War Eagles* and a condensed version of *Citizen Tom Paine* on my first day out. I did nothing on the following day but read and look at the sea. The color is the prettiest blue imaginable. When the waves break and the white foam forms with the blue, it makes a wonderful picture.

Finally, one day the ship's PX opened and sold 3 boxes of five-cent cookies, a lousy bar of candy, and a coke to the boys for 25 cents. At night one could buy cigarettes and soap.

We added an hour to our watches; so five o'clock in Rye is six on this ship. I reviewed *Retreat with Stillwell* and liked it a lot. Perhaps after the war I should become a book critic.

At seven o'clock at night everyone must be off deck and below in the hole. (As time goes on we are allowed to sleep on deck since "below" is terribly cramped.) I saw my first flying fish early one morn. They're tiny things that skim along above the water for 15 to 50 feet. The weather is getting warmer. I'm getting my summer tan now in October!

I was nominated for a policing detail and had to sweep the ship with some other lads. It didn't take long, and it helped break the monotony. In the afternoon I again took to the books. This time I gave my thoughts to *Valley of Decision* and *Life in a Putty Knife Factory*.

Saturday, we had something special. Everyone got another injection. With the ship tossing and rolling it's a wonder the needle didn't pierce my arm.

Washing is our biggest problem. We only have salt water, and you can't get any decent soap suds. Most of the dirt sticks to you or comes off on the towels. Shaving is also loads of fun. Some aren't scraping their whiskers but instead are growing beards. I have a tiny mirror so I can see to shave.

Our clock gained another hour on Monday and we're now 2 hours to the good. I played cards in the afternoon for a nickel a game. No one could do any steady winning. I ended up a plus seventy cents.

After much procrastinating, I began writing letters to everyone so that when I land I can mail them all out. Everyday I'll keep adding bits.

We have several newspaper photographers along with us, and one talked of his adventures in England, Africa, and Sicily. He wasn't bad and gave us useful hints in regard to purchasing articles abroad (Don't buy them.).

At night a fire drill was held. When the bell sounded everyone grabbed his life preserver and dashed on deck. The navy men loosened the hoses and shot the spray into the ocean. Several minutes later the all-clear signal was sounded.

I had guard duty for one full day. My first shift was from 12 to 4 in the afternoon; at night I was assigned deck duty to see all soldiers carried life preservers. The first two evening hours were fine with a full moon playing tricks on the water. However, the moon soon became lost and a deep mist set in. I could hardly see anything; not even the crew.

I had another physical exam. This didn't take very long, and then I turned to straining my eyes over *Wide Is the Gate* and *Mr. Winkle Goes to War*. Unfortunately, I wrote letters using dates and found I couldn't send any letter with date information; so I went back and rewrote my thoughts without mentioning the day, month or year. As a joke, I considered dating all my letters 1953, but I do not think the soldier doing the censorship would take this too lightly.

Days have passed. I stuck my arm out one day and received another typhus shot, making 3 since leaving Rye. That is my last injection on board ship. A couple of boys passed out. Wait until they go into action.

We've gotten so hungry that the ship's officer, with some strong prodding from the troops, decided to open up some C rations and gave us a can a day for several days. Boy did this stuff taste swell! We used to go to bed starving, but lately it hasn't been so bad.

The sea on this day in October is quite rough. Last night the ship tossed about something awful. Mess kits and canteens that were hanging up came clanging down. I woke up 4 times during the night with the rolling. It was blowing a gale and even in the hole it was cool. I put my overcoat over me to keep warm. I'm glad I took my sweater along but sorry I sent my shoes home. The lieutenant in the U.S.A. told us to ship them home, but most brought them along.

As we neared the coast of Africa, our ship's captain became more and more cautious. We were in dangerous waters with German submarines known to be lurking in the area. One night as I was falling asleep, I heard booming noises as U.S. destroyers tossed their depth charges into the ocean. We recognized U-Boats were nearby, but luck-ily none of them were able to catch us with our guard down. This was the only bit of action we encountered during the entire trip outside of the canteen bombardment incident.

My reading has dwindled away. At present I'm reading *The History of the U.S.* I got tired of reading murder stories, so I turned to the his-tory book for more intrigue.

Guess that's enough gas for now. Casablanca is just around the cor-ner so I'll say good-by. I'll write whenever I can.

Love to all,
Bob

CHAPTER 4

North Africa to Naples

On the Move: Casablanca to Oran

October 22, 1943

Dear Billy,

I've finally landed in Africa and have plenty to tell you. Of course in Africa you're bound to see plenty of Arabs. [A brilliant observation.] From what I can ascertain, the majority of Arabs appear to live in grass huts. Some plots contain grass walls erected around the houses. Inside the enclosures the Arabs keep their mules and camels. (Don't ask me where the women and children sleep.)

Along the highways you see Arabs plowing the fields. They don't use tractors or modern machinery but have only animals, generally two different varieties. It's not strange to see a camel and a horse, a horse and several cows, or camels and cows pulling the plow together.

The children run around without shoes, but then few Arabs own shoes. They try to steal our army shoes. Whenever you go to town you have to stay in pairs for the Arabs will do anything to get your clothes and shoes, even kill you.

Many of the children tend the sheep and cows. Whenever they see an American driving by they run out on the highway and yell "smoke." The Arabs fight like madmen over a single cigarette. In town they go around begging for a smoke; and when you take out a pack to offer them one, they snatch the whole pack and run away down the streets.

I've never seen anyone quite so dirty as these people. It would appear as though they never shaved or washed in their whole lives. Along the roads are water basins. The Arabs let their animals drink, and at the same time get their own drinking water from the same basin.

It's a common sight to see Arabs traveling on donkeys or in dirty old carts drawn by a donkey. Whenever an army truck approaches, they are required to pull off the road until the truck passes. Cars are seldom seen. The only gas available for consumption is Esso or Sphinx. Generally, people travel on bicycles or in horse-drawn carts. Bicycles, however, are the most popular form of transportation. The less said about trains the better.

Money is a different story; in fact we don't use American money at all. The French franc is the official currency in this part of Northern Africa. We had to exchange our American dollars for French money. As a rule the paper franc equals our two cents, thus a hundred francs is worth two dollars in American greenbacks.

Everything in Africa is saved. Wood and tin cans are carefully preserved. The old wooden boxes you throw away in the U.S. are put in bins for storage; nothing is wasted. It is impossible to buy wood for construction. The Arabs even try to steal our refuse at night.

Whenever we buy merchandise in the Post Exchange we have to produce our ration card. Everything is rationed too. Here are some of the things on our ration card—thread, ink, writing paper, soap box, nail file, towels, combs, shoe laces, lotions, and powder. Candy is a very precious article; in fact, candy bars (Milky Way, Baby Ruth, etc.) are not available. You can buy certain quantities of gum and lemon drops. The fellows who smoke find they can get 6 packs a week. We are also allowed 4 cakes of soap a month. Luckily, I brought a little extra over with me; so I'm set in this regard.

At present we are sleeping in tents holding 8 soldiers. There are no floors so to speak and quite a few tents have no beds. My bed is built of two by fours with chicken wire stretched across as a spring. Over the wire we put our tent shelters and blankets. Unfortunately, the wire is usually broken; so we place our barracks bag under the broken spots to keep from falling through.

It's pitch black when morning reveille is sounded. The moon and stars are still out. It doesn't even begin to get light until 7:30. We sleep at night in our clothes for in these unlighted tents it's too hard to dress in the morning. There is no electricity in our tents, but the army has given us candles to use. We are shown movies every second night. It is free and gets quite crowded in the outdoor theater. We sit on benches in the wide open spaces watching fairly new pictures. So far I've seen *Moon and Sixpence* and *Gentleman Jim*. We also saw a *Paramount News* dated November 11, 1942. (Almost a year old. Next week they have a talkie.)

All meals are served and eaten outside. The flies are mighty pesky, hungry, and numerous. In fact there are so many flying insects that they have to take a number and wait in line to feast on us. The Arabs love to deal with American boys. They can't buy clothes, cigarettes, and things but some of the soldiers do sell their pens, pencils, watches, rings, and lighters to them. The Arabs pay unbelievable prices for these goodies.

While we can buy a lead pencil for 10 cents or 25 cents in the states, we can get $2 or $3 for them in Africa.

The weather isn't bad. During the day the sun is rather strong and there is always a breeze. At night, however, it's a different story. It gets cold around 3 o'clock, and you use everything available to stay warm.

In town the Arabs peddle leather goods or rings. The trouble is they ask outrageous prices. For a small leather wallet they want 300 francs ($6.00). The soldiers generally cut the price in half and then bargain. You can get a pocketbook for 30 or 40 francs. They have the audacity to ask 35 francs for 3 postcards. When one Arab starts to show you his wares, all the others rush around and begin sticking articles in front of you. Then the fun begins.

Some of the French homes are very lovely. Usually, beautiful gardens surround the houses which are modern with winding staircases and flat roofs. Since wood is so scarce, these homes are built of stucco.

Food seems to be rationed. You can't buy much in town. Meals are served between certain hours in the "big" city. One eats lunch around twelve noon and supper at six. You can't buy a main meal between these hours. The only thing sold is wine and occasionally some sandwiches. I don't know what milk or cake tastes like anymore.

The camps feed so many soldiers that we receive only very small portions. If you're lucky you can go back for seconds but as a rule that's almost impossible. Naturally, this food comes from cans. One day when I had KP I really was able to fill my stomach.

Love to All,
Bob

First Class Accommodations: Cattle Cars

November 1943

Dear Folks,

Before I say anything I want to tell you that I shipped home $20 for my bank account and $5 for your birthdays. I won't be getting paid again until I reach my regular unit, and I don't know when that will be. Eventually, you'll be getting my bonds. I do receive a partial payment of $10 every 2 weeks; so I have plenty to hold me over. I don't spend much either.

I have another new address. I've been on a trip to Oran since departing from my week's stay in Casablanca and have lots to describe to you. From the start I realized our trip was due to be an "interesting" one. We were jam-packed into a four-wheel box car (similar to U.S. cattle cars). The only difference being that in this case we are the cattle. The car was constructed of rotten wood. There was nothing to sit on, no toilet facilities and the 4 open windows wouldn't close. Prior to starting, a water truck began filling the train's lister bag with water. Unfortunately, the hose broke and streams of water shot over my clothes, blankets, and pack. What a mess! The lister bag was too full; and when the train started forward, the rest of the water came over the sides and once again sprayed over me while I was desperately trying to sleep. That was the last straw. I blew up!

We were expected to sleep at night, but our quarters were so cramped that no one slept at all. Once during the night a steel helmet fell from the ceiling and hit me on the leg. I jumped sky high. I had strange legs all over me by morning. It took hours to untangle us. I could hardly stand up. Did my joints creak and groan! (Just like the 40' x 8' boxcar.) A great time was had by all.

Steam engines took us through beautiful countrysides. Whenever we came to a tunnel (and that was very often), the soot and smoke would cover us. We could hardly breathe, even though we covered our nose with a wet handkerchief.

At the stations where we stopped, the Arabs would rush out and try to peddle various items. We bought plenty of oranges for 5 francs and occasionally a sandwich for 5 francs too. We had to eat C rations the whole journey. Am I sick of them!

Every once in a while our train would pass a home with chickens and turkeys in the yard. Yes, believe it or not some of these homes had turkeys. (We also have "turkeys" on the train.)

The mountains were really beautiful. One scene reminded me of the Old West. We entered a huge valley surrounded by tall mountains. Green grass stretched across the floor, with cattle grazing amid the trees and running streams. How peaceful and quiet everything looked!

There were many deep gorges and valleys to be seen. We passed a canyon which could have been our own Grand Canyon.

We were traveling along merrily one day when all of a sudden a fellow fell off the box car and was left in no-man's land. Eventually, the MP stopped the train, and the poor scared fellow came running up. Was he glad to get back on board! I don't know what would have happened if the train had kept going. He would really have had a long hike.

I saw numerous human-inhabited caves along the route as well as many stone huts with mud-straw roofs. Outside these buildings you could notice dead animals that had been shot and would be used for food.

Hundreds of Arab children followed our train; the soldiers kept throwing them candies from our rations. They'd run after us for miles just begging for anything. Incidentally, going up hill our train only did 8 to 10 miles an hour.

There were no bridges built across the huge valleys; so the trains were obligated to go 10 or 20 miles out of the way to get from one mountain to another.

It's hard to describe which was the most beautiful place we saw. I've never seen anything quite so breath-taking. Everyone just kept looking at the landscape the whole trip.

Love to All,
"The Traveler"

Luxury Traveling Accommodations

Naples, Italy

New country; new camp—I still have a tent, but no beds, only hay mattresses. The first night it poured; my blankets and I got soaked. My barracks bag with my clothes was left outside and everything got wringing wet. Lucky me! We've just hit the rainy season.

Before leaving my last camp I had guard duty from 2 to 6 a.m. We carried loaded rifles and had to keep the "foxy" Arabs out of the lumber pen. If some did sneak through and wouldn't stop when we yelled, we'd blaze away. The hours from 1 to 4 a.m. are their infiltration hours. Was it dark and lonely! You could hear dogs barking and other noises, but no Arabs. The next day I stood guard in the afternoon from 1 to 8. I was supposed to be relieved at 8 but no relief appeared, and so there I stayed on duty. I was starving but could scrounge up only one lousy sandwich for supper.

I haven't had much time to do any writing. If I get a couple of free minutes I'll try to bring you up to date. With all my traveling, your letters from the states will never catch up with me.

We have movies here too but the darn rain keeps us in our tents. Candles or any lights are forbidden; so no writing at night.

The food isn't bad. We don't have to pull KP. Thank goodness.

Love to all,
Bob

CHAPTER 5

Italian Mountain Campaign

A New Home—"Sunny" Italy

November, 1943

Dear Folks,

As you can see from my latest address, I have finally joined my regular unit (3rd Infantry Division, 15th Regiment, Co K) as a rifleman. The weather is simply divine for ducks—it rains every day. You have read undoubtedly about the "lovely" Italian mud, but you have no idea what it's like! Your feet are always wet, cold, and full of mud. And to think I loved to make mud pies when I was a youngster and Mimi [mother] had mud facials.

Anyway, let me bring you up to date since my last letter. Upon leaving our camp outside the Naples race track, I and the rest of the contingency of raw recruits, were herded into open Army trucks and whisked away into the unknown. It started to rain and continued pouring the entire day. As we sped northward up the mountains, the temperature began to drop, the rain accelerated, and any vision of home vanished forever.

It is important to understand that in the infantry the buddy system is stressed. I met a young soldier from Champaign, Illinois, Russell Law, whose temperament was similar to mine. We both were playful, easy-going, fun-loving individuals with a great sense of humor, and we both felt invincible. It was only natural that we formed a close bond with each other. I must admit Russell and I liked to kid around; it helped relieve somewhat the stress of battle.

The mud mire of Italy was the key ingredient in Russell and me joining forces.

The truck we were riding eventually came to a screeching halt; the tailgate was lowered, and we were ordered to jump down (into the mud) and pick up our wet barracks bag. I located my bag, but I think Russell's sank in the quicksand. Anyway, his bag was listed as MIA (Missing In Action).

Let me enlighten you when I state Russell's loss was substantial. To the American doughboy his barracks bag was his home away from home. Besides all his personal belongings, the backpack contained blankets, sweater, entrenching tools, mess kit, rations, and the ingredients necessary to construct a pup tent with a fellow soldier. (Each soldier carried a shelter-half.) What a great beginning!

A jeep approached shortly thereafter, and a sergeant lined us up single file as our names were called out. A second soldier instructed us to follow him up a slippery, steep, rocky path. Twice I slipped and fell in the mud with my barracks bag. In frustration, I threw my helmet to the ground where it bounced off a rock and started rolling down the trail. Since Russell was traveling light, he pounced on my helmet and retrieved it.

And so was bonded an everlasting friendship. We became brothers.

You should have seen my bag; it was dirtier than the truck. Everything was filthy, mostly me. To make matters worse, the area where I had to pitch my tent quickly became a mud hole. Russell, I, and a few others ended up trying to sleep in a sitting position while the icy rain pelted us unmercifully. Speaking of inclement weather, I have to tell you gloves are a very precious article. You cannot buy a pair anywhere. A raincoat and leggings are other essentials.

Christmas came early this year when our PX rations arrived in November. This is one day every soldier overseas looks forward to. We received some real candy, compliments of Uncle Sam. Included in Santa's bag was a Tootsie Roll, pack of chewy candy, Hershey bar, 7 packs of chewing gum, a peanut bar, and cigarettes.

One of my first chores was to sew my 3rd Division insignia on my shirt and overcoat. I did a terrible job with my overcoat. I had to use pliers to pull the needle through; a seamstress I am not. I hate to admit it but I sewed my division patch on crooked the first time. Everything had to be ripped out and sewn over again.

You know, I haven't slept out of my clothes since leaving the states back on the 4th of October. I have to remove my shoes and leggings every so often because my feet are so wet and muddy. Only when I take a shower does just about everything drop off. However, you soon get used to this way of life; so I don't mind it too much. In fact it's so cold I would leave my clothes and mud on just to keep warm.

November 3, 1943

Dear Folks,

We built a fireplace in our tent but had to give it up. The smoke nearly killed everyone. It all went to the top of the tent, and we had to lay on our stomachs in order to breathe. It got so bad we couldn't see our hand before our face. We coughed and fumed and decided to call it quits. Do I need a hair cut! You can get them for practically nothing. In my last camp the guys were paying five cents in American silver for a cut.

I set a world record last week by keeping my shoes dry for two whole days. For the rest of the week they were soaking. The rain still falls (and not only in Spain).

I suppose by the time this letter finally hits you Christmas will have past. About a month ago back in Africa I sent you some V-mail Christmas cards. I wonder if you ever got them. You certainly can buy plenty of vino in this land. After pay day we really go to town. These Italians rip off the Americans too. They charge awful prices for wine and then when the soldier opens the bottle it's fizz water or something and not champagne. (This happened to one of the guys in my tent.) Real honest people these Italians.

Our shots still keep coming. I had another one added to the many previous ones. Let's see, that makes two hundred thirty-two to date, and still counting.

Hope you eat plenty of turkey for Thanksgiving. Oh for some of your cake and cookies! I have lots of shaving cream and such but no cake to be had. Christmas will soon be just around the corner, and so are the Germans. I'm sending you another V-mail Christmas card and trust it reaches you in time.

Love to all.
Merry Christmas,
Santa

Mt. Cassino, Mt. Lungo, and Mt. Rotundo

In Italy in the fall of 1943, a bitter series of battles for the mountain passes around Mount Cassino had been going on for two months. The 3rd Infantry Division had crossed the Volturno River and was facing extremely heavy resistance in the mountain ranges (German Winter Line or Gustav Line) south of Mount Cassino. The Germans controlled the heights overlooking the entire valley from Mts. Cassino, Lungo, and Rotundo. Supplying food and ammunition to the troops was a major problem. Even the sure-footed mules carrying food, water, and ammunition had trouble negotiating the steep hills. Toss in twenty-four hours a day of torrential rain/snow and you can readily smell trouble. The action had become stalemated. Every attempt to seize the slopes of Mt. Lungo and Mt. Rotundo was met with intense and costly resistance.

I thought I had successfully adjusted my life from that of civilian to that of soldier when I left the USA for the battlefields of Europe. I recognized that the demands made on civilians were entirely different than those on combat infantrymen. Although I was apprehensive when I joined the 3rd, I was totally unprepared for life as a frontline combat infantryman. Make no mistake; the baptism was quick but painful. No more beds with pillows, sheets, or blankets. No roof or overhead structure to keep you dry, no chairs to sit on in front of the fireplace, no electricity, lights, heat or air conditioning units, no bathrooms, no flush toilets, no hot water showers nor hot food eaten on plates. No snacks; no raids on the refrigerator. The morning hot cup of coffee passed into oblivion, as did a balanced menu. Instead of a car, bus, or cab to transport you to the next town, you had the privilege of walking there, single file with a rifle and a pack on your back. No restaurants, fast food facilities, or supermarkets along the way. Your attire never varied; no dress-up code required. No worries about clean air, global warming, gas/oil shortages, or noise restraints. No political debates. No radio, books, newspaper, telephone, movies, or other forms of communication were available on a daily basis. A peaceful night's sleep was a dream long since forgotten. You had the privilege of being shot at twenty-four hours a day, with extremely limited medical assistance at your disposal. Mail call became one of the highlights of the day. "Dear John" letters increased as the days slipped by. After the "mail call" cry, the second most heard call was "medic." (Someone was down or injured.) Your friends were quick to disappear; new ones were always waiting for you. The freezing rain never stopped. Prayer became an integral part of one's life. Your guardian angel was always at your side.

One of the most useful pieces of equipment the army bestowed upon a combat soldier was the helmet. Besides the protection it offered, the helmet served as a wash basin. Water was poured into the inverted headpiece, and a splash or two applied to one's whiskers or face. A new man emerged! Towels were non-productive; shirt sleeves replaced them. Money was practically useless. Your life was not your own. Death became your constant companion. You dreamed of returning home but never fully believed it would happen to you. Your main objective was to stay alive and perhaps sustain a "million-dollar" wound, which would remove you from further combat. You kept remembering the good 'ole days and waiting to hear the latest rumors. Will the war ever end? The list was endless.

As soon as we new recruits (casualty replacements) joined K Company, we were immediately indoctrinated into the art of modern warfare. I was selected as they say in the army, along with others, to be part of a combat patrol to infiltrate enemy lines and reconnoiter the slopes of Cassino—"City of the Dead" as our newspaper, the *Stars and Stripes*, called it. One evening

> we left our base camp at 5 p.m. in the pitch blackness and did not return until 7:30 a.m. the following day. I never told you but on this particular patrol we actually reached the base of Cassino and were fortunate enough to collect and pass along some valuable military information regarding German troop locations. During this patrol we were so close to the enemy we could see the Germans digging their tanks into the ground. For a while it looked as though we were not going to make it back safely. Our artillery had to be called in directly on us. When our shells started falling, the Jerries kept their heads down and dove into their foxholes. At that moment we quickly picked up our baggage and disappeared into the night. All in all we were 14 hours behind German lines. When we finally returned to Mt. Lungo, we were totally exhausted. At first it seemed impossible to even think of climbing to the base camp, but somehow we made it up the steep inclines.

It doesn't take anyone very long in combat to graduate from recruit to veteran. Russell and I made the jump in a matter of hours. Our next patrol was several days later. We both volunteered to take part in the action. Our objective was to cross the nearby river and gather information on the whereabouts of the German regiment facing us. We had just waded the icy river when suddenly we noticed

> the Jerries were bringing in their tanks, and we had nothing but rifles to throw at them. A quick decision was made; let's get the hell out of here. The river afforded us the protection that we needed; so we hit the river

for a second swim in a matter of hours. Brrrr! What a way to go! No matter how you analyzed the situation, swimming was better than being wiped out.

The weathermen in Italy had a relatively easy job predicting tomorrow's weather. Every day it was rain, rain and more rain with a sprinkling of snow. Fighting in the mountain passes around Cassino was extremely fierce; progress was often non-existent; intense German counter-attacks could be expected momentarily.

Moving into Position

San Pietro, Italy

San Pietro was the key link to the entire Liri Valley and had to be captured at all costs. Mt. Lungo and Mt. Rotundo loomed in front of San Pietro and sheltered the city. Attacks on these German strongholds were without success until November 10, 1943 when after days of intense fighting the 3rd Infantry Division finally penetrated the German Winter Line and captured Rotundo and Lungo.

> The Jerries continuously counterattacked our positions, and many times we were in doubt whether we could hold out. The wounded had to be carried on stretchers in the pouring rain all the way down these rocky mountains; so you can visualize what a tenuous situation we were in.

"Greater Love Hath No Man Than This, That a Man Lay Down His Life for His Friends"

A few days after the Germans vacated San Pietro, our platoon lieutenant ordered Russell and me to meet him at K Company headquarters with our rifles. We were going to have the privilege of accompanying him on a daytime three-man reconnaissance patrol to search for Germans in "no-man's land" as the valley was known. The area was infested with mines, abandoned German equipment, and blood-spattered corpses. Gunfire could be heard in the distance. All that was missing was Allied troops.

Our lieutenant, carrying only a sidearm, was off and running up the twisting mountain trail at the crack of the starter's pistol. Russell and I, each toting a handicap in the form of a nine-pound M1 rifle plus ammo, struggled to keep up with him.

> As we tiptoed through the mine fields, we could see in the distance a high mountain with a monastery sitting on its peak. It was Cassino Hill.

No Germans were spotted during our sortie. However, while returning to our base camp, it was decided for security purposes to return by a different route. We selected a fairly smooth roadbed to head back. As we continued along, the ravine became narrower

(8–10 feet in width) and the banks on the side of the road grew in heights to 10–15 feet. Eventually, we were stopped in our tracks. In front of us, blocking our passage, was a mass of fairly loose barbed wire, criss-crossing the road and attached to the ravine's wall sides for some 10 feet in height. On the roadbed was a partially hidden massive landmine with wires intertwined with the barbed wire. We had no tools to cut the wire; we did not want to retrace our steps; we all agreed to work our way forward gingerly. Fortunately, we did not realize the gravity of the task.

The criss-crossing wire appeared easy to stretch without affecting the wire attached to the mine. Russell and I held the wires apart which allowed the lieutenant to slip through. He slid through, dashed down the road, and disappeared from sight. One down; two to go.

Quickly, the pressure began to mount! It was Russell's turn to challenge death and beat the odds. I would bring up the rear. (If there was to be one.)

I'll say one thing; Russell was very confident. Unfortunately, Russell's rifle and jacket had different ideas. Within seconds the rifle and Russell became attached to the barbed wire. The situation was deteriorating fast. Besides keeping the menacing mine stationary, I had to pry Russell and his rifle apart from the wire. Slowly, I removed the rifle from his shoulder and placed it on the ground. Next problem was Russell's jacket. By holding the barbed wire firm and at the same time gently extracting the jacket from the wire, I was able to free him. Two down; one to go. By now the intensity of the situation had reached monumental proportions.

My first move was to pass both rifles and jackets through the obstruction to Russell. He accepted these gifts and stood by to assist me. I managed to slide through but not without a terrifying moment; my shirt became snagged! Although swiftly resolved, it seemed like an eternity before we were safe and sound. Remember, while the barbed wire was being patiently massaged, the Lieutenant, Russell and I were at one time or another staring the mine squarely in the face. Talk about stress!

Russell wrote his and my parents about this incident. He felt I had saved his life. It was always a joke after we got back safely. However, at the time there was a distinct possibility one or both of us was going to be blown to bits. I never will understand why the mine did not explode. I had a feeling it was my guardian angel who was at my side, working overtime.

From that day forward, Russell and I were inseparable. We only parted ways when Russell was later wounded and returned to the United States. His parents reached out to my mother and father and practically adopted me. Whenever they could, the Laws sent me care packages and continuously contacted my family to make sure I was at least still alive. During the war I always found time to write them. Our bond never faltered. They felt I was a "hero" who had remained with their son when he needed me the most; now it was their turn to be with me.

> Dear "23,"
> While writing this letter, I am rereading some of your letters. I see where Mr. Taubeneck predicted that war would be over by Easter. I don't know how right he is but these Jerries are tough. They are well-entrenched in these mountains around Cassino and have slowed down the whole Fifth Army. One thing I am glad is that the fighting is over here and not in America. I've seen towns much bigger than Rye leveled to the ground. The smell of decaying bodies is awful. These civilians in Italy really know the meaning of pain, anguish, and fear.

It should be borne in mind that fascist Italy was a member of the Axis countries along with Germany and Japan.

> So Auntie is still handing out ration books. Do you think you will ever get finished with rationing? Probably not until after the war. Anyway as long as America has enough oil, they're ok. These poor people that depend on coal will find it tough this year.
> Don't worry about me. I am fine; but not my watch. I doubt I will ever get it fixed over here. I cannot understand what's wrong. I know for sure it is not wound too much, but it refuses to work. Too tired, I suppose. Just when I need it the most. I'm as disappointed as you with Tiffanys. It is certainly a swell looking watch. Unfortunately, it can only tell the correct time twice a day.
> I had my tooth fixed; in fact I had it fixed permanently so that it will never bother me again. The tooth had been hurting for quite a while; the dentist solved my problem and any future problem by extraction.
> I still don't care for coffee but will drink tea if I am really thirsty. Speaking of thirst always reminds me of Mt. Lungo. On Lungo, water

was at a premium; we often had to fill our water canteens from the water that had collected in shell holes brought about by German artillery shelling. The taste of the powder in these holes was wicked, but water was precious to come by, regardless of taste.

Love,
"Gunga Din"

It has been said that chocolate is the downfall of many a man. Russell and I were great lovers of anything that even closely resembled chocolate, so you can recognize the troubles that could arise when Russell and I were mixed with an ingredient known as "pure chocolate."

Let me set the stage. K Company was dug into a rugged mountain facing Mt. Cassino. Digging a foxhole was not one of our strong points. Add a steep, rocky mountain with little or no soil, and you can appreciate the problem. However, in this particular instance, Russell and I had outdone ourselves in preparing our foxhole. We were able to scratch a shallow foxhole three feet deep, almost enough to provide safety from enemy shells. With our "make-do" background, we decided to complete our construction by building upward a few additional feet rather than the conventional downward thrust. By piling rocks around our residence, we were able to double the protection coverage (6 feet vs. 3 feet). Ours was a fortress to be admired by all. Two canvas shelter halves were spread over the opening and provided us with protection from the elements (rain not artillery shells).

A few days after completion of our "Cassino Home of the Future," Russell and I volunteered to go on a night patrol behind German lines. Once our mission was completed, we staggered back to camp completely exhausted. Both of us felt the need for a pick-me-up. A hot chocolate sounded great! We had a small stove in our foxhole. By covering the stove with our helmet prior to lighting, we deduced we could hide any tell-tale signs from our enemy.

Our company commander had issued strict orders forbidding any fires or matches being struck after dark. The Germans were watching for any such point of light on which to fire their 88mm cannons. On the other hand, Russell and I could envision the hot chocolate touching our lips. Oh hell, let's go for it! The stove was covered and lit. Within seconds, we heard the shell with our name seeking us out. The world exploded at our doorstep. Dirt and rocks were strewn over the mountainside; our canvas coverings were ripped to shreds. It felt like our brains were scattered to the four corners of the world; the ringing would not stop. Most importantly, we were not wounded. Eventually, blessed sleep descended on us.

The following morning we were awakened by a fellow soldier checking to see if anyone was alive in our foxhole. We were alive and kicking, but each had forever lost all hearing in one ear. Neither Russell nor I ever discussed this close call with our parents or friends. The Germans had seen the glow from lighting the stove and had zeroed in on us. Thank goodness they miscalculated by a foot or two. A miss is as good as a mile, they say! We agreed!

Usually, patrols consisted of a small group of soldiers sent out on a reconnaissance mission. After being briefed as to the purpose of the operation, everyone was furnished with a password of the day, for example "Black-White."

You must understand there is always a gray area that the patrol is exposed to upon return to the Allied sector. The patrol must identify itself when so challenged. In this instance the American challenger would call out "Black" and the patrol for identification would respond "White," thereby clearing the safe passage of the patrol.

On the other side of the coin, Russell and I had been exposed to situations where the Germans tried to infiltrate our lines. They would attempt to trick us by yelling, "I am American," and hope we would not open fire. You cannot make a mistake in wartime; it could cost you your life. No password reply could only mean one thing. Our rifle/machine-gun fire would quickly resolve this problem.

1943 Draws to a Close

After 59 days of continuous, bitter mountain fighting, the 3rd Infantry Division was relieved. Our job of capturing Mt. Lungo was successful and the 36th Infantry Division was relieving us. We were headed for a well-deserved rest.

Home Sweet Home

The losses the 3rd Division sustained in the Cassino struggle were staggering. Many of our depleted infantry companies had only 20 men leaving the hill whereas 180 soldiers per company had originally attempted to scale the heights! Our regiment required over 700 men to refill our ranks.

As for the 36th Division, they were in time pushed off Lungo by the Germans; battle plans had to be rewritten. By year end 1943, Lungo was recaptured by U.S. forces.

In memory of this campaign, a huge temporary cemetery was built at the foot of Lungo where the fallen soldiers from the 3rd and 36th Divisions were laid to rest. After World War II the remains of these soldiers were moved to a permanent site known as the Sicily-Rome American Cemetery and Memorial, located approximately 40 miles south of Rome in Nettuno, Italy.

Rest Camp

Dear Folks,

I finally received several letters from you. It was swell to hear what was going on in Rye. I received 8 letters in all—6 from you and 2 from Gene.

I'm glad you've fixed up the playroom in the basement. Perhaps by next fall I may be around to use it again. Don't tell me you actually got the screens down? Why Daddy, I'm surprised at you. I figured you'd save vital time and energy by leaving them up another whole year. Isn't it wonderful to be twenty again? You say you have painted the dining room and cleaned and waxed the floor. Did you do only the woodwork or did you remove the wallpaper and really fix the place up? This undertaking a/k/a Miracle on Twenty-Three Oakwood Avenue must rank up there with *Miracle on 34th Street*. Are you being considered for an award?

You don't need to send your letters by airmail since they won't arrive any faster. When I received your old letters they were all stamped up. I sat down and read the letters from the oldest to the latest one—Nov. 16, 1943. Fortunately, one fellow in our tent receives *Reader's Digest* so we have plenty to read but there is not enough daylight.

The other day I wrote Alyce Sloat, Ann, Chickie, Gene as well as the rest of the gang who write so regularly. I've been to a few movies here at the rest camp. I saw *Janie and Mrs. Parkington*! The funniest of them all was *Abroad with Two Yanks*. I also received the socks from Mary Stuart that she mailed me first class some time ago. They are grand to wear and are the best that I've had since arriving overseas. When one pair gets wet (which is almost a daily occurrence) I switch to the other pair.

Every day the Russian news sounds better. This is one topic that is discussed quite regularly in our tents after chow.

Chickie contacted me and sent me a copy of the Dodgers' newspaper. Also went to the town beer joint and saw *Frisco Sal*! It helped pass the time until guard duty.

Love to All.
Have a great Christmas.
Tell Santa where I am,
Bob

On Thanksgiving Day, we were treated to beans and a salmon cutlet for lunch and C rations (stew) for dinner. However, on Friday, a feast was presented, and we did receive a small taste of turkey and gravy. It was outstanding and brought back great memories of home and family.

Our weekly shower comes on Thursday. Once a week, we get fairly clean and the rest of the time we are dirty clean. After a brief washing, you can discern a patch or two of white skin under one's uniform. Cigarettes are sold for 5 cents a pack as compared to the Liberty ship's 45 cents a carton. What a difference compared to the prices you must pay in the States. Have a Merry Christmas. I might not be able to write you as often as I have in the past. Duty calls.

Love to All,
Bob

CHAPTER 6

Anzio to Rome

3rd Infantry Division Timetable in Anzio to Rome Campaign

Date	Description
1943	
Nov 17	Relieved from Mt. Cassino combat by 36th Infantry Division.
Dec 28	3rd Infantry Division to lead amphibious assault on Anzio. Training commences; new recruits arrive. Anzio Objective—outflank Gustav line; capture Rome.
1944	
Jan 19	Practice landing—Salerno. A complete disaster!
Jan 21	Set sail from Naples for Anzio; 96,000 American and British troops
Jan 22	3rd Infantry Division (reinforced) and British 1st Division (reinforced) land; area almost free of enemy forces. Initial objectives met; jeep reconnaissance patrol reaches Rome without opposition and returns; regrouping; beachhead buildup; port area clearing commences. 45th Infantry Division in reserve.
Jan 23	German reinforcements pour into region; commence counterattacks. Allied supplies continue to arrive; delays encountered unloading ships.
Jan 24–25	Allied units slowly push inland. Germans now have eight divisions facing outnumbered Allied forces. Front lines are everywhere, even rear areas. No safe haven on beachhead.
Jan 26–29	Corps Commander orders a temporary halt to Allied offensive. Germans prepare for counterattack to eliminate the beachhead.
Jan 30	Allies renew their offensives. 3rd Infantry Division and Ranger battalions spearhead assault on Cisterna. Heavy opposition. Rangers ambushed; rescue attempts by 15th regiment falls short. Of the 767 rangers involved in assault only 6 return.

Date	Description
1944	
Feb 3–7	Germans launch 1st major counter-attack. Bitter fighting; Germans forced to retreat; staggering German losses (approximately 5,400 soldiers).
Feb 12	Ten German divisions on beachhead; approximately 120,000 troops vs. Allied Forces of 96,000. Major decision had to be made. Were British and United States war offices going to write off the Anzio campaign? Were we Anzio soldiers looking at total destruction? Another Dunkirk?
Feb 16–19	Second major German attack. Three days of fierce battles. All units badly decimated. General John P. Lucas relieved of command of VI corps; General Lucian Truscott of the 3rd Infantry Division takes charge of VI corps; U.S. artillery barrages devastating to Germans. Drive collapses for Germans.
Feb 29–Mar 3	Third huge German attack ordered by Hitler himself commences in an effort to push Allies back into the sea. Major thrust against 3rd Infantry Division. Horrific losses on both sides, especially 3rd Infantry Division's 7th and 15th regiments. Artillery was instrumental in eventually breaking the attack; 3,500 German casualties. Allies counter-attack and recapture lost territory. Germans go on defensive; lull begins.
Mar–Apr	Stalemate; depleted ranks filled by new replacements; wretched conditions—rain, mud; both sides stage raids and artillery duals; daily patrols. Newspapers compare Anzio battlefields to World War I trench fighting where soldiers stood for hours in trenches/foxholes with water up to their ankles. Often the enemy was only a football field's length away.
Mar 3–10	15th Regiment moved to rest camp; showers, new uniforms available.
Mar 28	3rd Infantry Division relieved after 67 days of continuous front-line combat.
Apr 11	Moved back into combat position. Outposts established; combat patrols dispatched nightly to probe enemy defenses. Allied divisions utilize "psychological attack"—loud speakers directed at enemy lines urging surrender.
May 1	3rd Infantry Division prepares for offensive to smash out of beachhead. Seven full Allied divisions ready.

Date	Description
1944	
May 23	Allied push to Rome commences. Had to cross extensive German minefields; heavy fighting. 3rd Infantry Division battle casualties on this day alone were 995; believed to be the largest number suffered to date by any single U.S. Army division in one day in World War II (official 3rd Infantry Division records).
May 25	Beachhead ceased to exist. Units head north; objective—Rome.
May 28–29	Badly needed replacements arrive.
Jun 4	Reconnaissance units reach Rome; city mostly abandoned by Germans.
Jun 5	Rome secured. Entire 3rd Infantry Division relieved of front-line duty; prepare to garrison Rome.

World War II's Greatest Blunder?

Prior to reaching our rest area after leaving Cassino, rumors began to spread like wildfire. Was the war winding down for the 3rd Infantry Division, and were we being readied for occupational duty in Rome? Such an undertaking would be too good to be true, but we held out hope as to its authenticity. Unfortunately, it did not take long for the bubble to burst. Within days, word came down from headquarters that the 3rd Infantry Division would take part in an amphibious operation behind enemy lines sometime after mid-January 1944. Destination: Anzio, Italy, an obscure, relatively flat strip of land, 30 miles south of Rome which, hopefully, would be the key leading to a quick capture of Rome. There would be no rest for the weary. A three-week preparation timetable was established; two reinforced divisions (one American and one British) would spearhead the initial amphibious assault with the 3rd Infantry Division leading the U.S. with all three regiments plus a battalion of Rangers. Our 15th Regiment was awarded the honor of being in the first-wave assault group. We commenced training on techniques utilized to attack and destroy coastal fortifications and pillboxes, and how to cross minefields. However, thank goodness no one foresaw what the future held in store for us. The port of Anzio would have its name written in blood; there would be no swift capture of Rome. The campaign fought at Anzio would go down in history as one of the most violent, vicious battles of World War II.

A Block Buster

January 14, 1944

Dear Folks,

I forgot to tell you I got a very slight pay boost of $4.80 a month, starting the first of January, 1944. The army also promoted me to PFC (Private First Class).

I received a card notifying me of your blood donation given in my honor. It came in the mail the other day with letters from you, Red, Gene and Ruthie. Ann sent me a great unbreakable mirror in her care package. That was one gift I really needed. Our campaign ribbons were distributed last week. I'll probably never wear them but I have them anyway.

Training—Amphibious Landing

Time was not on our side as 1944 opened its doors. Our division had been allotted a mere three weeks to prepare for Anzio. There was a strong feeling among the troops that we would be going into battle short of equipment and loaded with recruits who did not have sufficient training. On January 19, 1944, just three days before the scheduled Anzio landings, we had our first and only dress rehearsal. That was a night I will never forget! After censorship was a thing of the past, I sat down and recorded the chilling events. Plainly stated, the rehearsal landing in which we utilized British ships, was a complete fiasco! The landing crafts were launched in high seas so far distant from our objective that it took three to four additional hours to reach the beaches. Many an amphibious craft was swamped and sank in the rough waters. Not a single battalion managed to land at the correct time or location. Confusion abounded; everything was chaotic! It was a complete disaster! Fortunately, it was only a rehearsal, except for those who perished in the vicious seas.

Dear Folks,

Troubles started early the night of our rehearsal landing. The sea was extremely turbulent. At two in the morning, we struggled down the cargo nets of our British transport ship with full pack and rifle and boarded the bobbing landing craft. The waves continually smashed over the bow of our tiny boat. Due to the fact that we transferred to our landing vessel much too far out in the ocean, our trip to the shore was twice as long. As time passed the waves seemed to become rougher and rougher. We were quickly soaked to the skin and sick as the devil. Everyone was seasick. Gradually, the boat started to fill with water, and we began to wonder whether or not we could make land. Some landing craft turned back, but we kept heading in the general direction of the shore. The soldiers in our platoon removed their packs just in case we went down. I felt sorry for those who could not swim (Russell was one of the non-swimmers). The stress on them was even greater than on those who could swim. It wasn't long before we heard cries for help as boats and crews began to sink beneath the angry waves. To make matters worse our landing craft was overloaded. In view of the circumstances it was impossible to render assistance to those floundering nearby. The waves were so high I doubt if we could have located anyone in the water. Hours later our craft reached solid ground. I was never so glad to touch land as I was to hit the shores of Salerno. We were so weak by that time that it was pitiful! We lost tons of equipment, landing crafts, and men. This was only the beginning of a series of blunders.

January 18, 1944

Dear Folks,

I guess I'll have to write you a V-mail letter instead of a long one because I don't have the time anymore. I received some wonderful Christmas boxes. The Rye Committee sent me a great box of cookies, candies and cake. There were hard candies, a box of Schrafft's peanut brittle, fudge, cakes, and some huge cookies. It was most impressive; nothing went to waste.

Love to All,
Bob

This was to be the last letter I could write for sometime. The Anzio invasion took place four days later. From then on, it was pure hell for four long months. Shortly after the Anzio invasion, I traded my rifle for a light machine gun. The firepower of this gun was tremendous! I could wipe out a squad of Germans before they knew what hit them. I must confess the final days prior to the invasion were an agony of waiting. Would this be a bloodbath for the first wave? The strain began to tell on everyone.

D-Day Anzio: January 22, 1944

Room for One More

Go! Go! Go!

The invasion of Anzio went like clockwork. Our first-wave assault crafts landed in the early dawn. The enemy was completely caught by surprise; objectives were quickly met. There was little opposition; only a few stray Germans in the vicinity. The road to Rome was open. It was ours for the taking. I was in the first wave of the attack. As I crouched in the landing craft and headed toward the enemy shore, I felt all alone. What would I meet when the ramp opened? Would I be running directly into a hail of bullets as most predicted? How many of us will get off the beach before being cut down? Is this the end? I could only pray.

Our craft hit bottom about 10 feet from shore. The ramp dropped down, and it was time to go. I held my breath and plunged in knee-deep water. I kept low and tried to keep my rifle dry. Couldn't see what was going on. I was loaded with ammunition; backpack felt like it weighed a ton. To my surprise and relief no Germans were visible although in the distance I could hear machine-gun fire. If anyone had been waiting for us, they could easily have cut us to ribbons. During training we were taught to get off the beach as quickly as possible. We wasted no time scrambling off the landing craft and heading inland within a matter of minutes. Confusion abounded on the beach; we didn't know where to go; we didn't know what was next. It was nightmarish for a while. Numerous German bunkers and gun positions had been erected; few were manned. The Italians on the beachhead informed us there were no enemy troops between Anzio and Rome. Unfortunately, delivering supplies and additional soldiers to the beachhead became extremely difficult (shortage of amphibious assault landing crafts). Instead of walking into Rome, headquarters decided to move cautiously. As a result the Krauts brought in reinforcements yesterday while we waited until tomorrow.

I will always believe hundreds of our men needn't have died if the VI Corps had only hurried a mite more. We in the front lines hung tenaciously to this small piece of Italian land waiting in vain for more men, supplies, and orders to move forward.

To fully understand the impact of the decision to take no offensive action in the period immediately following our landing, let me explain that the terrain on the beachhead was ill-suited for combat. The entire area was flat by nature with numerous ravines dotting the countryside. There were no major towns on the beachhead area other than Anzio/Nettuno. The 3rd's objective, the Mussolini Canal, was considered the eastern boundary of our beach perimeter. Far beyond the beach was a mountain range known as the Alban Hills, highest point 3,100 feet. From this ideal vantage point the Germans could look down our throats and saturate the entire countryside with intense artillery fire. Consequently, daylight movements were held to a minimum. In addition two major highways leading directly to Rome bounded the Alban Hills. These hills were, therefore, an objective that demanded immediate attention.

While cautious General Lucas fiddled, as the early Romans used to say, the GIs were burnt. Quickly, the Germans, under General Field Marshall Albert Kesselring, poured men and supplies into the region. Within thirty-six hours the initiative passed from the Allies to the Germans. We had to dig in to hold our positions and prevent being annihilated; foxholes and dugouts were interconnected; mines were sown; and an approach area was covered with artillery, mortar, machine-gun, and rifle fire.

Life on the Beachhead

On January 30, 1944 the 3rd Infantry Division combined with elements of two Ranger battalions commenced an attack on Cisterna; the 15th regiment was to pass to the right of Cisterna and cut the main highway. Little did we know as we moved forward through a series of small ditches and into the face of intense fire that we were doomed for failure. Standing in front of us, poised for a pending counter-attack in a few days, were the elements of thirty-six German battalions!

As you probably read, Mussolini reclaimed the Anzio-Nettuno area in the 1930s. The Italians filled in the land and dug a series of irrigation gullies/canals. Our K company's initial mission this day in January was to capture the area west of the Mussolini Canal. It was at the Canal where we met our first real enemy opposition. The Germans zeroed in with their artillery guns and gave us hell. We kept inching forward and running directly into machine-gun nests. Casualties were staggering. It did not take long for the Canal to start to run crimson (blood). Our throats became parched; there was no fresh water to quench our thirst; we removed our steel helmets, filled them with the bloody canal water, and drank. You could feel the dirt and taste the blood as you swallowed the water, but no one cared. It helped our thirst and that was all that mattered.

Every place you looked you saw wounded or dead G.I.s. It seemed impossible to escape death. We were slowly being annihilated. You could see the terror in your buddies' eyes. In one instance a German shell landed directly on a litter crew of 4 men carrying a wounded soldier. The five bodies were scattered to the four winds. The fighting became so intense that no one could attempt to carry out the wounded. When the shells screamed in, you hugged the walls of the canal, prayed, and waited to feel the hot metal as it ripped into your body.

The Mussolini Canal was exceptionally deep where we were pinned down. This plus the facts that (1) we had pushed a long way up the canal and (2) the artillery barrages never seemed to stop, made it almost impossible to bring in medical assistance. It was terrifying beyond comprehension! Eventually, we (survivors) were all able to fight our way out of the canal and reach firm ground not in the direct fire of the German artillery.

The next night a Ranger battalion moved through our disseminated ranks to capture Cisterna. The Germans with their tanks were waiting for them as they were for us (K Company) and sprang a devastating ambush on the Rangers. German battle lines were formed as an inverted U. When the Rangers entered the U shaped ring, it closed tight; communications were cut. The German tanks and machine-guns opened up on the Rangers at point-blank range. All hell broke loose. We made a desperate attempt to rescue the Rangers but the enemy swarmed all over us, forcing us to retreat. You can imagine the carnage! Inside 8 hours the Ranger battalions were eliminated from the face of the earth.

A brochure prepared in the U.S. Army Center of Military History stated that "of the 767 men in the two Ranger battalions, only 6 soldiers eventually returned to Allied lines."

As I remember the terrible events of that day, I cannot help but recall parts of Lord Alfred Tennyson's famous poem "Charge of the Light Brigade." Change a few words and you can vividly picture the Ranger battalions being slaughtered.

> Cannon to right of them,
> Cannon to left of them,
> Cannon behind them.
> Volley'd and thunder'd;
> Storm'd at with shot and shell,
> While horse and hero fell,
> They that had fought so well
> Came thro' the Jaws of Death,
> Back from the mouth of Hell,
> All that was left of them,
> Left of six hundred.

Hide 'n' Seek

Since the Germans held the mountains and the Allies were on level ground with no place to hide, the four-month struggle for survival quickly became a no-win situation. Blood flowed like water; diarrhea was running rampant (pardon the pun); the Germans shot down on us with their big guns. They could pick out your foxhole and blast away. In the daytime we were forced to crouch in our foxholes with water at times lapping at our ankles. Life was miserable. Our clothing and blankets were seldom dry.

Often animals were caught in the German barrages and killed. Once a cow strayed by our outpost and paid the price. As the days passed, the body of the cow became bloated and the stench unrelenting. Finally, one night a group of us dug a hole some distance from our foxholes and disposed of the carcass, or so we thought. Another job well done. The following morning the Jerries spotted the new digging and immediately commenced shelling the area. As fate would have it, the Germans hit their target (the cow) and sent it flying (over the moon). The only satisfaction was a cleansing of the air.

On Anzio Beachhead

Dear Daddy,

You have heard of boys writing home from foxholes; so now I am doing the same. Artillery is zipping over my head but I haven't lost a single hair. Before going on I want to tell you about a story from the Christmas *Reader's Digest*. It tells about flyers and how they continually pray for help. That article set me to thinking. Perhaps some day I'll write a similar article to the *Digest* about we infantry boys. Believe you me we often pray to Him and ask for His protection when we go out on dangerous missions. I heard my sergeant say a few words which I will never forget as long as I live. It was just after one of my close pals was killed; everyone was in a bad mood. The sergeant walked around muttering, "The Lord giveth and the Lord taketh away." That really touched me down deep. Boys who seldom went to church back in the States are just as devout as any of us. They look forward to meeting the chaplain and having him say a few words. Over here in death's row, you get to know the meaning of death and of fear, but after you say a prayer or two, your fear subsides somewhat and death doesn't seem so frightening. Many a time I have lain on the ground with a gun cuddled against my stomach and prayed to be brought safely through the night.

Gene White and Bob Thornton are mighty lucky lads. It doesn't appear as if Gene will ever come overseas. For Thornton's sake, I hope he never has to be thrown into front line combat. You cannot imagine what it's like until you have been here for a while and had a taste of real tough living conditions. I live in foxholes all the time (except when moving into the attack of course). I do not remember the last time I washed thoroughly. Anyway, I've learned to dig a real homey Anzio foxhole complete with running water (rain), living room, radio and coal stove. (Oh ya!!) Speaking of "coal," it gets awfully cold at night out in the open. My feet freeze! As a rule I sleep a little, stand guard, go on patrol and then sleep a mite more. Some fun! Some life! Some excitement!

I'm looking forward to receiving all that candy you are sending me. My comrades got a great laugh over your suggestion that perhaps the Red Cross has a candy bar or two they could sell us. If the Red Cross does get any, they certainly never would pass them outside their own offices. They have been around a couple of times with doughnuts but that's all. They completely disappeared after that. Miss you and think of you always.

Your loving son,
Bob

Dear Folks,

I must say your care parcels are a great help. I had 2 packages fly in the other day; both packages were sent 3 or 4 months ago to K Company and hadn't arrived until just now. One box was in perfect condition but the other must have been used as a football. All the cookies were smashed, but that didn't matter because we were so hungry. We had crumb zoop.

Since I'm telling you things that I will never forget, I may as well mention this story. Night-time in Anzio was the only time we could get out of our foxhole. If you were wounded you could not be patched up until dark. One night we collected all the bodies of soldiers in our company who had died the past few days. We placed them in a pile near the Mussolini Canal. Suddenly, a low whine was heard and a shell landed right smack in the middle of these 29 dead men. Their bodies were blown to bits. The army would never find out who they were. This is one of the reasons many parents received telegrams saying so and so was missing in action. These soldiers just disappeared; it would take years, if ever, to track them down and find out what actually happened.

Love to All,
Bob

Three Strikes and You're Out

February 1944 was a critical period for the Allies and the 3rd Infantry Division. Ammunition and rations were stocked near our defensive sites. We were well entrenched and had completely mined and created a wall of steel (barbwire) around our positions. Headquarters had established separate resistance battle lines; one company from each battalion remained in the forward position followed by the second and third (main line of resistance) lines some 200 to 300 yards to the rear. If the first line was breached, the second and third lines could be defended. (In other words, the first line might be labeled as being expendable.)

The Germans were, likewise, deeply dug in. Only 96,401 Allied soldiers stood between them and the beach at Anzio-Nettuno. It was time for the Germans with their estimated 10 divisions (120,000 men) to crush the Allies. The first counter-attack commenced February 3rd, 1944. We could hear the tanks rumbling as they moved forward; artillery barrages covered the beachhead; the Luftwaffe was always nearby. There was no safe haven on Anzio! Bitter, bloody fighting ensued. When the dust had cleared, the Germans found they had been unable to break through our lines. Losses on both sides were staggering!

In anticipation of a second blitzkrieg, our artillery emplacements, commencing February 15th, pounded the German front lines. The Germans responded with a saturation shelling of the front lines followed by a diversionary infantry assault against the 3rd Infantry Division on February 16th near Cisterna. Fortunately, the muddy terrain limited the effectiveness of the German Panzer tanks. Our air, naval, and artillery strikes combined with small arms and tank fire turned the tide. After three days of intensive fighting, the Germans were forced to pull back once again. The crisis had passed; many German units had lost most of their firepower. Our Allied 5-day losses were severe, totaling 3,496 killed, wounded, or missing. Everyone was feeling the intense strain of battle. Several tried to report to the hospital on the pretext that they were nervously incapable of further combat.

Anzio Foxhole

Dear Folks,

I'm awfully glad you sent me that article about Tom O'Keefe. He's lucky to be in the army mail service rather than with me in the frontlines. What he says about the boys' eyes lighting up at mail call is true. Mail is the grandest thing to receive when the going gets tough, believe you me. Keep 'er up!

I see Bernie Balls was a radioman in the Air Corps. Regardless of what they say, the infantryman in the front-lines has the most terrifying, savage, everlasting, and dangerous job of them all. I would gladly trade shoes with Bernie any day. I know he had it tough at times, but his life was nothing like mine, being exhausted in a wet, cold, muddy foxhole in Anzio with shells landing all around. You swear the following one was going to land in your hole. Once it went off and you were not hit, you would breathe a sigh of relief and get ready for the next shell. After several minutes of intensive shelling, you'd think your nerves could stand no more; but soon it would lift, and you could gather your senses, or whatever was left of them.

Bernie has battle stars which is great; we have them too. The company handed them out to me some time ago. I wouldn't have ever remembered them if I had not seen the newspaper article you sent me. We wear these stars on the campaign ribbon. I have another ribbon but never bother wearing it. The main thing is to do your job and return home after the war.

Oh well, why write anymore on this war. No matter where you are overseas, it's not easy. Everyone is making a sacrifice and has things to squawk about. Frank Sloat, Bernie and O'Keefe probably have had narrow squeaks. They are all heroes; in fact anyone is a hero who goes to battle for freedom against an enemy he has never met, never knowing when or what will happen next.

All my love,
Bob

February 17, 1944

Dear Ole Gang,

In your letter you enclosed the clipping about O'Keefe eating C rations on Christmas. Well, that's exactly what I ate too. I can hardly wait for the day when I'll be able to sit down to your wonderful roast beef dinners with cake and milk!

Recently, I decided to try once again to get that darn watch of mine going. To my amusement, the arms began to flap after I gave them a few lusty taps. At first it would go and stop but now it only marches forward. I've got my fingers crossed.

Old Jack Frost really nipped my toes this year. They are numb as can be and ache like the devil. (Guess I'm getting kinda old.) Will I be glad to see the warmer days and shorter nights. Perhaps the rain will let up ever so slightly. Russell and I haven't lost our sense of humor altogether. We continue to play tricks on our compatriots from time to time. Our latest was to lob mud balls at our neighboring foxholes, wait for the splatter, and let out a blood-curdling sound as if the mud ball had found its mark on one of us. Anything to relieve the tension.

Incidentally, I am still trying to discover the therapeutic value of Italian MUD. I realize scores of women back home rave about mud, but really. . . .

February 24, 1944

Dear Non-Combatants and Paper Readers,

I have some real news for you—your Christmas package finally arrived with the wristlets. The chocolate bars I distributed among my comrades and myself. Did they taste good! That ole watch of mine stopped again. I'm going to give up on it.

My stomach has been doing tricks these past few days. I don't think I've ever been quite as sick. Finally, I had to get some medical assistance. I'll be fine in a day or two.

Love to All,
Bob

On Anzio Beachhead
February 25, 1944

Dear Folks,

Once again my hair has begun to grow. I think it's longer than yours. The only good thing is that it keeps me warm, but it certainly collects dirt and mud galore. What tangles! My hands seemed to have changed color. They are black as pitch. No matter how hard I try to dig the dirt out, it's no use. I'm afraid I'll have to wait until I return to the states and start getting KP before they'll actually begin to look white again. Russell and I sleep together in our foxholes for added warmth and try to always stick close to one another on night patrols into no-man's land. I must confess we love to accompany new recruits on patrol behind enemy lines. Just picture Russell on patrol in the pitch blackness suddenly pulling up short and whispering to a replacement "what was that?" or "did you hear that?" We all freeze in our tracks, the tension mounts and we strain our ears to listen for the imaginary sound Russell had "heard." No one dares to take another step. Finally, we move on ever so slowly, our eyes searching the darkness for some movement. So far so good.

All my Love,
Bob

This would be my last letter back home for several weeks. The final German counter-attack was about to begin. Our world in Anzio would soon explode violently. The 3rd Infantry Division would be forced to bear the brunt of the attack. Once again the fields were about to be covered with dead and mutilated bodies.

The Final German Assault:
February 28–March 1, 1944

The last major German counter-attack on Anzio took place on February 29th when the Germans unleashed the full power of the German Army. The attack was directed straight at K Company, 15th Regiment of the 3rd Infantry Division.

To begin with the 3rd Division was in a defensive position. By the luck of the draw K Company was assigned the frontline position (expendable) at "Hells Corner" with I and L Companies in reserve. There are 3 infantry battalions in a regiment and each battalion employed one company up front and 2 in reserve. On our left flank was G Company and on our right C Company.

The morning of the twenty-ninth opened with an earth-shattering artillery barrage by the Jerries. The dreaded 88-millimeter guns with their high-powered shells screamed at us. Then the Krauts began moving forward with tanks and infantry. God! Look at them all. "G" Company was caught asleep, and their positions quickly overrun. Assistance was needed immediately.

Russell, I and a few others in our weapon's platoon were summoned to a nearby farmhouse, which acted as our company headquarters, and informed our neighboring battalion was in dire need of additional firepower. Although I was supposed to join Russell, at the last moment there was a change in plans. I returned to K Company, and my replacement, Emil Fiffick, connected forces with Russell.

Here we stood, one company (115 men or so) against approximately a battalion of Krauts (600 more or less); our left flank was exposed; the Krauts moved behind and cut us off from all support forces. Right then and there we became engaged in one of the bloodiest battles of the beachhead. The German superiority in manpower enabled them to break our company's first line of resistance. We were fighting for our lives and every shot had to count. There would be no tomorrow. With Germans swarming all around us, the assault quickly became an intense hand-to-hand battle.

I was in a machine-gun outpost. My buddies and I kept firing, reloading, firing, reloading. Adrenalin juices took over our bodies. It was as though we enjoyed slaughtering every German in our sights.

We couldn't stop; the Germans would not let up. We annihilated an incredible number of Germans; they retreated, regrouped and came at us with a fresh battalion. All day the battle raged. It was nothing to have a Kraut hand grenade land near you, and in a split-second for you to throw it back at the Germans before it exploded. Hand grenades were one of the best weapons we had at our disposal that fateful day.

Each platoon became a fighting unit of its own with the Jerries at times between our own platoons. We could not call for artillery because the Krauts and Americans were too close together. No one was coming to our aid or to relieve us; the companies behind us had to hold the line at any cost, even if our company had to be sacrificed.

Around the barbwire in front of our machine-gun nest, the dead Germans began to pile up as wave after wave were beaten back. However, our company was having high casualties as well, and we could not afford the losses. Our lines began to buckle by continued fanatical attacks. We killed Germans at point-blank range. Somehow or other we withstood the frenzied German efforts and drove them back with heavy losses. By night the intense attacks stopped, and we had time to treat our wounded. It seemed that every soldier in our company had at least a nick or two, some much more than others. We were exhausted, without medical supplies, ammunition, or water, but weren't beaten by a long shot. The majority merely licked their wounds and kept fighting.

In the morning, with our ranks depleted by heavy casualties, the Germans came charging again, and it seemed for a while as if the whole beachhead would collapse. The noise was horrendous! Hitler was throwing everything at us in his all out move to drive us into the sea. Things never looked darker than they did on that gray morn. Would our prayers be answered?

Fortunately, the Germans could not breach our fortifications. We would not bend. It was simply a case of kill or be killed. The bitter assault kept up for 3 days, and at the end of the battle we knew we would never lose Anzio. The ones I really felt extremely sorry for were the recent replacements; they had such a tough time. The majority were quickly wounded or killed; you never knew them and would never see them again. One night 28 new recruits joined our company and by dawn, there was only one left standing.

The dead covered the fields and already were beginning to smell. A local truce was declared in spots, and the hundreds and hundreds of lifeless bodies on both sides were carted away to the burial grounds.

The Germans lost so many men they could never throw another such attack at us. I think our division alone smashed 3 German divisions; and, remember, it was the 3rd who held the center of the beachhead and whom the Jerries threw their main forces at during the assaults. Within a week, everything was quiet and all that remained were memories that would last us a lifetime. The question was how long was a lifetime. A day; a week; a year?

It's funny, the Germans had so much going for them and we had so little, but still they couldn't conquer us. They sent tanks at us, and we had nothing to throw at them except artillery and guts. They fired point-blank at our foxholes, but it wasn't enough. They sent their men right into our ranks, but still it wasn't enough. They tossed their finest and best equipped soldiers at us for 3 consecutive days but it wasn't enough. They couldn't lick us no matter how hard they tried because the American soldier is made of something down deep inside that can take anything the others throw at him and still come back for more.

When it was all over, the ones like myself who walked away alive had aged terribly. Many, including yours truly, had either white hair or found their nerves shattered. Of course, I was still a fool at heart but my hair was white. My guardian angel had done a magnificent job for me.

With Love to All,
Bob

Little did I know that during this terrible bloody, three-day battle, my close friend Russell and I would be called upon to part company. Russell was badly wounded. Fortunately, he was evacuated to safety. In general during this engagement many of the wounded who could not be moved except by ambulance never lived long enough to see the hospital.

The following account of this battle was written by Russell:

We walked up the road for about one-half a mile to a bridge over a shallow ditch. There we met a sergeant from the other outfit. He directed us to go down the ditch and follow him another half mile to the location of their 30 cal. machine-gun emplacement. The gun was fully loaded with a belt of ammunition; there were only two extra boxes of ammunition nearby. The sergeant warned us to keep our heads down but to watch out for the Germans that were directly in front of us. It had rained most of the day and continued through the night. Our foxhole was about half full of water.

Our artillery shells were landing very close to our location. We spent the night watching and listening for any enemy movement. Emil was on guard and I was dozing. Toward morning I was awakened by the heaviest shelling I had ever heard. We could hear the artillery going both ways; it was landing close in front of us (American) and to our rear (German).

Finally, the shelling stopped from both sides at the same time. We decided to see if the enemy was stirring. There in front of us was a German officer running at top speed at our position. This was too easy; I calmly pointed the machine-gun at him and squeezed the trigger. His arms flew up in the air as he fell forward on his face.

Emil spotted a unit of Germans on our left. He kept firing his rifle, and they scattered in all directions. I swung the machine-gun around to face them and pulled the trigger; it fired once and quit. What luck! We examined the two extra boxes of water-logged ammunition and attempted to reload; the belt would not feed through the gun. It seemed like this was a good time to fall back to another machine-gun emplacement that was across the ditch. I had no idea why it was unmanned.

The new location would be fatal to Emil when an aerial burst hit nearby, wounding Russell in the right shoulder and instantly killing Emil. By afternoon the battle subsided somewhat and Russell was able to make his way up the ditch and back to headquarters for medical assistance. I was devastated to learn Russell had been wounded. We had survived so many dangerous, terrifying, hair-raising attacks together. The end was brutal and abrupt. My life was never quite the same after his departure. I kept thinking it would have been different if only I was there.

Mrs. Law was not kidding when she mentioned how lucky I was that day. (My guardian angel would not let me go.) I must admit I was fortunate but I've had 3 even luckier, if you can call it that, escapes. Some day I'll tell you about them, and we can laugh and forget them.

All my Love,
Bob

Here They Come

It was in the days following the third and last attempt by the Germans to crush us that in a weak moment of tomfoolery on my part, I almost lost my life. Several of us were in a machine-gun outpost directly overlooking the German lines approximately 50–75 yards in front of us. Every evening as darkness took hold, one of us had to return to our main line of resistance and pick up rations for the squad. On this particular night it was my duty to gather rations. Before going on, let me explain that at times my sense of humor was somewhat warped. This evening I gathered up my rifle and headed back to pick up our gourmet delights. A sudden and brilliant inspiration hit me! We were all totally exhausted from our recent bloody battles with the Germans. It was good to be alive even though our living conditions were wretched. Why not add a little humor to the situation and capture my own men! It would be a relatively simple thing to do. All that was necessary would be for me to walk about 100 yards away, turn my helmet around so it would look like a German helmet, and yell "Achtung, cummon zee here." I was sure they would give up. So-o-o, with my mind made up, I returned in the darkness barking orders in pig German, and demanding surrender. Within a few seconds, I had captured my own men. With tears rolling down my eyes,

I turned my helmet around and confessed I was the culprit. Eventually, we all had a great laugh until one of my buddies said, "Lynch, you are crazy. I was going to shoot you, but I was too tired of this war to bother." At that moment I realized my mistake. "What fools we mortals be!"

Today I Will Lay Down My Life for My Country

Dear Auntie and Company,

I have another Anzio story. I'm afraid they are all the same in that the ending never changes. Draw up your chair and listen to the story of a close friend of mine, a tough sergeant, who said he'd never go home, and didn't.

It was February just 5 days before we were to be relieved of our forward positions on "Hells Corner." That night our sergeant was officially told inside a week's time, he would be heading home for good. (Sergeant had been in 3rd Division prior to WW II.) He was excruciatingly happy at the news. In a matter of minutes his joy rubbed off on his squad. We all became intoxicated with his happiness. Unfortunately, when the five days were up, our company was not relieved as anticipated. Instead, for some unknown reason, we had to remain at the front for 2 more nights before falling back into our second line of defense 300 yards to the rear. [To this day I do not know why the sergeant wasn't relieved immediately and brought to safety. He wasn't indispensable.] Anyway, when the old sergeant learned we were not to be relieved, he sat down and told us he would never go home now. He said he knew down deep in his heart that he would stay here forever in Anzio. We all kidded him and told him to forget it. Nothing would happen to him. He was going home.

It was just getting dark on the sixth night when the Jerries threw a terrific artillery barrage at us. I was watching out of my foxhole when I saw the shell hit; the explosion was deafening. I knew it was close; too close for comfort.

When the shelling was over, we checked to see who was injured. I walked slowly toward the spot where I had seen that last shell go off. The foxhole in which the lieutenant and sergeant had been staying was now nothing more than a big shell hole. All we ever found was a watch the sergeant wore on his wrist. You can't imagine the feeling that engulfed us. We were devastated!! We had lost him!! Shock waves kept permeating through our bodies. His words kept coming back to us, "I'll never leave Anzio if I don't get relieved on time." The relief was two days late! Only two days late! He might have lived to see 90 years if our company hadn't had to stay at the front 2 extra days. Two days is such a short time, but it wasn't short enough. It takes only a split second to lose your life!

Love to All,
Bob

A New Chapter Begins—Stalemate

Life on the beachhead was slowly getting back to normal which is more than I can say for us survivors. Our lives would never be the same again. Would the terrible scars of battle heal? The nightmares are still real. How and why did I survive?

Signs of spring were in the air, and the weather was turning warm. With the heat came swarms of insects (no tourists) to visit Anzio.

Anzio Beachhead
March 9, 1944

Dear Ole Twenty-three,

Boy, am I anxiously awaiting the end of this winter! Probably sometime this summer my feet will warm up. Anyway, now I have some nice, heavy wool socks to keep my "stubs" hot.

I'm having a hard time writing this V-mail. This is my first opportunity to write in weeks but I don't know what to gab about; I'm so tense. I expect some letters soon; haven't received any for several weeks. I'm fine. My sick stomach has disappeared completely, but I've lost my appetite in the exchange. Nerves.

I had some swell cookies the other day. One fellow got a package full of cookies. Of course, you know how I hate cookies. They were delicious!! Everyone shares his care package with others. I and a few others receive the bulk of the cookie boxes.

March 27, 1944

Dear Auntie,

I received several pocketbooks from Uncle Sam which I read in my cozy foxhole. I managed to read *Action of Aquila, The Yearling, Gentle Annie,* and *Suds in Your Eyes.* Reading certainly helps make the day a little more pleasurable, and some of the books are really good. It's too bad I didn't take a speed reading course in college. I'd be able to finish the sentence I'm reading before that artillery shell I hear whistling towards me hits nearby.

My wildcat watch has again decided to get up steam and do a little running. Yes, it's on a rampage and is ticking off the hours like nobody's business. How long this will last I have no idea.

I finally received a letter from Gene and Chickie but your old letters are still on the way. Personally, I think they are coming across the Pacific, around Africa, and up to Italy before finally locating me in my foxhole.

The 2 lb. box of Fanny Farmer Christmas candies has not reached me. I have given up all hope of ever seeing the package. (I'll bet Santa ate them; he couldn't find me.)

All my Love,
Bob

A Slight Reprieve

On March 28, 1944, the 34th Infantry Division relieved the 3rd Infantry Division at the front lines near Cisterna. We had been in frontline combat for sixty-seven continuous days, under deplorable conditions. The stress of battle was beginning to show on everyone's face. Although we were totally exhausted, morale remained high. Replacements again began to filter in. Life appeared to be improving, ever so slightly.

For two full days we did nothing but shower, relax, shower again, and sleep. It was glorious! Unfortunately, all good things must come to a close, some too soon. After our rest, we moved into a nearby training area in preparation for our pending assault on the German minefields and emplacements. There was no use kidding ourselves, the worst was yet to come.

April 2, 1944

Dear Folks,

Santa Claus brought me a great surprise; all your packages were dropped by. Nearly a dozen of these pennies from heaven found my foxhole. The heavy woolen socks from Mary Stuart that I waited so long for this winter finally arrived. I probably won't be able to thank Mary Stuart right away; so you'll have to thank her for me. It was Christmas in springtime. You know she sent me two pair of heavy woolen socks. Ruthie mailed me gloves and a few cookies. Your fantastic box of cookies, wool knit cap, and candy were unbelievable. Then, to top the day off, I received peanut butter and Hershey bars from Mrs. Janssen. Our squad had a great time testing all the cookies and candy. Thanks for sending everything.

I am in excellent condition (not like poor Gene). I can't understand what happened to my stomach, but I gradually recovered by myself. I certainly wish I could have written more often these past months but as you know it was simply impossible. The fighting has been so intense! Whenever I did manage to get my hands on a V-mail, I wrote you. Some fellows have sent their campaign ribbons home in regular letters; so I'm attaching mine to this page and hope you'll get it.

Love to All,
Bob

April 2, 1944

Dear Mom and Dad,

Say, what is this talk about men overseas in the infantry getting a Pfc. (Private First Class) rating? As of yet, it hasn't gone into effect with us because many of the old men are still down in the pay books as Privates. Eventually, I suppose, the law will be in place, but you know how slow things are overseas. Lots of my pals are getting base pay but are hoping for this slight increase. Raises and promotions in the combat infantry are practically non-existent. Often you receive the title of "Acting Squad Leader" from your captain but the promotion never follows.

The packages I received must have been sitting around for months. I passed the Hershey's out to everyone in my platoon and divided the cookies with the gang. Everyone who tasted your cookies loved them, and only two cookies in the whole lot were broken.

Today is Palm Sunday, and I received a great surprise from the mailman—over 50 letters from everyone in Rye. I hadn't received any letters from you since Feb 12th and here it is April 2nd. I am re-reading each letter again and again. It is great fun! Joan Reilly (Ann's sister) wrote me a long letter the other day. She wanted to know what I thought of this "soldiers vote" bill. I have so little time to think of anything in combat that I don't see how I can vote intelligently. No one in our squad knows what the candidates' platforms are or much of anything about the men themselves. Most of us have enough on our minds to think about rather than worry whether we will be able to vote or not this coming election.

My buddy, Russell, is still in the hospital. I am looking forward to his return, although I'm not too sure he will be back. For his sake, I hope not. One could get hurt in this job.

You asked me about mass on Sundays. The Catholic boys have a little Sunday missal which they can read. Naturally, the chaplain cannot say mass when we're in combat, but we see him whenever we can. The 15th Infantry Regiment has their own chaplain, a Captain Moore by name. He's a real nice guy; very popular.

All my Love,
Bob

Easter Sunday

Dear Folks,

Somehow this doesn't seem like Easter. It's just like any other day except that I went to church (one of the very few times this year that I could attend).

I received some letters that you sent me the beginning of October. Thank goodness for that saying "The mail must get through." (They don't say how long, though.)

We obtained our monthly PX rations which consisted of 3 candy bars (getting better for it's usually one or two bars), some gum, and about 4 pieces of writing paper per person.

Chickie wrote and told me all about Buddy's illness. She mentioned she is sending me a box of goodies which I'll keep my eye (and mouth) out for. She's been great corresponding with me. Her sister, Ann, is always asking about me. They are very loyal.

Happy Easter to All,
Bob

Preparation for Spring Offensive: Training

Every infantry company has at least several soldiers fully trained to fire the bazooka. This weapon is an anti-tank gun which is fired from the shoulder. One man loads the missile and the other fires the bazooka. Bull's-eye!

Our command felt it would be advisable to have more than one bazooka squad handy when the final battle to break out of the beachhead is underway. Pfc. Hudson and Pfc. Lynch (myself) were chosen to trade in their light machine guns and ammunition for a bazooka. Our "extensive" training consisted of learning the mechanics of this weapon and firing the bazooka once. I'll never forget my one and only shot. I placed the bazooka on my shoulder and aimed it at the objective some 100 yards away. Hudson loaded the weapon and tapped me on the shoulder to let me know it was fully operational. The trigger was pulled and the missile flew forward perhaps 20–30 yards before gently landing on the ground and running ahead another few yards. Not too auspicious a start, I must say. However, beggars can't be choosy; Hudson and I were the new bazooka team for K Company. God help us!

April 22, 1944

Dear Residents of 23 Oakwood Avenue,

By the date, you will see it has been a year since you last fed me a home-cooked meal. It has also been 3 months of pure hell since we were first introduced to Anzio. Since 22 is such a popular number, I'll probably be 22 (age) before I return to good ole 23. Also, I was born in '22.

My sweater has taken a terrible beating. It's beginning to change color (muddy brown) and show the wear. I have it on 30 hours a day [that is not a misprint]; so you can understand why I will have to retire it one of these days. I hope I won't need another one; the war can't last forever, can it?

All my Love,
Bob

April 24, 1944

Dear Folks,

Let's see now—what shall I talk about today. I have my driver's license with me, and it runs out late in May. I wonder if I have to renew it since I'm "vacationing" over here. I hope I can let it go another year and renew it without taking another test. I'd like you to find out what the whole story is in this matter.

Naturally, my watch has decided to take a rest again. Yep, that's right. The darn thing isn't going; but don't worry. Some day it will wake up and start ticking.

I had a hole in my tooth that I had to have fixed. You can imagine how difficult it was to get away from our foxhole. The dentist drilled for a couple of minutes, and then I was on my way back to the front. I can't stay away too long; they'll miss me.

Love from Anzio Beachhead,
Bob

The Days Dwindle Down

Our time in the rear for training was over before we knew it. It was time for the 3rd Infantry Division to return to the front lines. By mid-April, we were back at what we did best—killing Krauts. During the month both sides staged limited probing raids and patrols, and had extensive artillery duals. Our combat patrols slipped out nightly to harass the Germans. I often volunteered for these nightly patrols. One in particular comes to mind!

There was a patrol on Anzio that I was supposed to join that seemed impossible to accomplish. If we had left as scheduled, we probably would never have been heard from again. Our hierarchy called the patrol together one day and gave us a briefing on what was to be our mission. We were to infiltrate 12 miles behind Jerry lines and blow up a vital bridge on Highway #6 (Rome to Naples highway). To cross the range of mountains we had to wade through infested mine fields and somehow slip by the enemy defenses. This meant doing super-human feats like climbing over barbwire, crossing streams and most of all finding our way to the bridge in the dark with no guides, street signs or anything. There were about 8 of us "hand picked" for the job, most of whom were new recruits. Our rifle grenadier had never shot the weapon and knew absolutely nothing about it. Other patrols had tried to penetrate the enemy lines on 4 previous occasions and had either been completely destroyed or had just disappeared in the darkness. Anyway, at the last moment, the major called us in and told us we weren't going. No patrol was sent out to blow up this bridge again. However, we did capture it <u>intact</u> on our march to Rome.

Love,
Bob

May 3, 1944

Dear Civilians,

I just heard from Gene, and I notice the ole boy has returned to Rye for 16 more days of vacation. Hasn't he been lucky? Our PX ration has come and everyone received several precious candy bars. Now the government is going to give us beer or cokes every so often. This is the first time for the Anzio boys.

Hold onto your seats because you are going to receive a real surprise. Believe it or not, I actually had fresh eggs for 2 days. Yes, for two unforgettable days every soldier got 3 eggs. We have never had fresh eggs since the invasion; so you can imagine how astonished we were. I remember back home I would never look at an egg, but over here it's entirely different. They taste so-o-o good!

I've heard from several N.Y.U. boys since you gave Doug Ward my address. Sam Jones was stationed at the Maryland College with Ward. Lucky guys!

Probably by the time you receive this letter, Mother's Day will have passed. Next year, we'll be together to help celebrate Mother's Day, but this year the "boss" (U.S. Army) wants us to work.

Love to All,
Bob

May 14, 1944

Dear Everyone,

I wish these pesty flies would stop trying to play hide 'n' seek with me. One tries to hide in my ear and the other zooms in looking for him. They have a jolly good time at my expense.

Before I tell you the news, I want you to sit down and take a long breath. Now, lean back and relax. You're looking much better. You'll never believe it, but my dear uncle (his last name is Sammy), aka Uncle Sam, bestowed upon yours truly a Good Conduct medal. I am not too sure what it's for unless it's because I have been on my best behavior these past few days. The lieutenant even nods to me when he sees me instead of running and hiding. I know it won't keep up like this forever, but I'm enjoying the comradeship while I can.

All My Love,
Your "obedient" Son,
Bob

May 20, 1944

Dear Folks,

I haven't had time to do any reading in many a moon, but recently I got my hands on some old *Reader's Digests*. When I say old, I mean OLD. Several were from 1940 and most of the authors kept saying our boys would never fight on foreign soil. I think I'll write and ask them what everyone is doing over here. Maybe we are lost. Who knows?

In the spring of 1944 when the fighting was spasmodic, the Germans introduced us to their latest invention: a 280mm German railway gun which they zeroed in on the beachhead and proceeded to fire 550-pound shells with terrifying results. The gun was securely mounted on a German truck, hidden in a railroad tunnel, and dubbed "Anzio Annie"; the casualties from this instrument of death and other German artillery attacks were incredible. Official records for March 1944 showed that "shrapnel caused 83% of all 3rd Infantry Division casualties during this period."

As soon as I heard we would be leaving Anzio, I placed another "For Sale" sign on my foxhole. There is no question it was a quaint, cozy room with an indoor pool. No one seemed interested, and I left without obtaining a single bid. It was the "location" I guess.

To a Precious Few

How does one approach the prospect of almost certain death? Most of us wrote our loved ones knowing it might be the last letter they would receive from their son overseas. We reminisced about the years gone by and the opportunities lost. We worried how our parents and friends would react when they learned the news. How would we die? Would we die? Was our sacrifice in vain? Would there always be war?

The topic of death was utmost in the mind of every combat soldier on Anzio as the day approached when the Allied forces would commence their final push toward Rome. The date had been established—May 23, 1944. The enemy knew the attack was coming; their artillery was focused on every possible Allied target. The fields to be crossed were thoroughly mined; snipers, obstacles, and machine-gun nests were everywhere; the Germans were well entrenched; their tanks dotted the countryside. Casualties were projected to be exceedingly high, probably one out of every two infantrymen would be killed or wounded. A strong sense of pending doom filled the air. It was extremely difficult to believe any of us could overcome all these obstacles and make it safely through this assault. I prayed and asked my guardian angel to once again watch over me. He heard my cry.

Crossing the Valley of Death

He guides me along the right path;
He is true to his name.
If I should walk in the valley of darkness
no evil would I fear.
You are there with your crook and your staff;
with these you give me comfort.

—Psalm 23

On May 23, 1944 at 0545, the final attack to crush the Germans surrounding Anzio began. For 45 minutes our naval ships and Allied artillery blasted every known German position on the beachhead. Our mission (K Company) was to by-pass Cisterna to the southeast and cut Highway 7, the main German retreat route.

I had already prayed, bid farewells to my friends, and wished them a safe crossing. Now it was time to meet my destiny. I felt all alone as I moved forward with my eyes glued to the ground in search of mines. (It was not until many years later that my eyes were opened and I realized I was not alone. The good Lord was at my side.) One cannot imagine the sheer terror which accompanied us as we crossed the valley of death. Enormous sacrifices on both sides were about to be made. So began one of the bloodiest single encounters fought by any division in World War II. In the space of three days every German in Anzio was killed or wounded or had retreated!

The Onslaught

Anzio Beachhead

Dear Folks,

The day we began our path northward toward Rome, we suffered the highest number of casualties in a single day yet known in this war. The machine gun, mortar, automatic rifle fire and mine fields were wicked! And we had to walk straight through them. The German 88-millimeter shells kept screaming at us. Death was all around. I saw a body blown at least 50 feet in the air. He looked like an old sack of clothes coming down. You heard soldiers screaming for medics or holding their torn, mangled leg with blood spurting. One buddy showed me what was left of his leg, and he thought he was lucky to get away so easy. It only cost him a leg while others had to pay with their lives. Evacuation was just as rugged, and many died along the way to the hospital. There were literally thousands of anti-tank and anti-personnel mines strewn all over the area by both sides. It was hard to miss one. In addition, the snipers were as thick as flies. (Italian flies.) They clipped our wings but we never faltered.

Blasting a Sniper

The attack was to feature a revolutionary idea in tank warfare. Each regiment had assigned to them a battle-sled team of sixty men. One medium tank pulling twelve armored sleds with an infantryman on each sled would cross the minefields and, hopefully, set off the mines, thus clearing the way for the infantry. A great idea on paper; however, to my knowledge, our tanks were quickly knocked out. The extensive minefields had to be crossed without any outside assistance, other than prayers.

Heroic actions and sacrifices were ongoing throughout the day. My sergeant was an old-timer who was informed by his lieutenant prior to the pending assault that he was being relieved of duty and would not have to cross the fields. He flatly refused to leave his squad—"my squad," as he put it. He had come this far and wanted to be—"with my men." (Most of his group were green recruits.) I yelled to him to watch out for the mines as his squad and the squad I was assigned started our separate ways. That was the last time I ever saw him. Later in the day, I was told the young recruit with him panicked and tripped a mine, killing both instantly.

Communication during battle was always a major problem. While crossing the minefields in single file, a message was often passed back from soldier to soldier. As the intensity of the assault grew, it was inevitable that a call for "bazooka man up front" be sent out. The message was relayed from the beginning of the line all the way back to the end where Hudson and I were stationed. (Apparently, the regular bazooka men merely relayed the message back.) There was no one I could pass the message to: Hudson and I were it. We crawled to meet the lieutenant who "politely" informed us that a "Tiger tank is in the vicinity," and it was up to Hudson and me to "knock it out." We were expected to creep through the minefields and locate/destroy this humongous roadblock. Quite an undertaking for anyone, especially a team with our "experience" firing the bazooka. Our only hope was for a lucky shot before the tank "saw" and blasted us into oblivion.

Hudson and I crept forward for what we felt was an eternity. We realized we had to pop up sometime and look for the tank. As we lay on the ground, we loaded the bazooka so we could get several shots off in a hurry. We fully expected to look directly at the tracks of a Kraut tank. I took a deep breath and called upon my guardian angel. I was ready, he was ready; it was now or never! Quickly, I popped up on my knees and took a fast look. To my relief, the German tank had moved elsewhere. Believe me, I was not going to track it down! The odds were too one-sided in the Germans' favor. However, my mind was always ticking. Two novices, Hudson and I, had been literally pushed into this seek 'n' destroy situation. Why not turn it around to our benefit? The noise from our bazooka shells was heard back at our lines. Little did anyone know that Hudson and I were merely firing the missiles harmlessly into the air at an imaginary tank. The shells exploded upon contact with the ground. We returned to report "mission accomplished" and received a "well-done" pat on the back. Our squad could now move forward directly into the hail of enemy machine-gun and mortar fire originating from the nearby Kraut-held woods and houses.

On one occasion our column stopped in a deep ditch to rest. Three of us, including myself, climbed to the top of the ditch to look over the vast wheat field to see what possible German targets we could spot. We stood straight up and picked out an enemy machine gun nest far to our right. As anyone will tell you, it's foolish to expose yourself too long because sooner or later some sniper will get you in his sights. We could hear the bullets singing around us; but we thought we were invincible, and so like statues we stood there an extra second or two. Time ticked by. Suddenly, our buddy in the middle dropped to the ground. I gathered he saw something important and didn't want to be seen. A second later I knew that a sniper's bullet had found its mark. He was fortunate in that eventually he was nursed back to health and returned to civilian life.

Dear Folks,

Whenever I remember Anzio, there is one story that I cannot forget. It was during the first days of the beachhead when the Jerries counter-attacked one of our outposts at night. Our troops were literally caught asleep. The Germans overran our entrenchments, killing any soldier they found in foxholes. I was with K company's main body several hundred yards behind our outpost. We were powerless to come to their aid and by morning it was too late. Our company was given orders to pull back about 500 yards and begin setting up our permanent defense line. The foxholes where our boys lay in undisturbed sleep were soon an area to be known as no-man's land. German artillery shells would continuously land nearby. Whenever Russell and I went out on patrols at night, we had to crawl around this spot where only the dead lay. The morning of the breakthrough to Rome [May 23, 1944], we passed by this shelled-out area. The soldiers' bodies were still in their holes just as we had left them 4 months ago. The cold had preserved their bodies so they appeared to be sleeping. I knew several of my friends were there, but I couldn't recognize anyone.

There is so much I could tell you about this tiny beachhead that it would take letters upon letters to complete. Incidentally, as I was looking through my wallet, I came across one of our propaganda sheets that we shower on the enemy. The Germans shoot them at us too. A few of the popular German "I surrender" ones mentioned Roosevelt's speech that "never again shall our boys set foot on foreign soil." At Christmas time we had some really touching ones from Germany. They showed a little girl praying for her daddy's return, and at the same time a German sniper's bullet cut him down. The Germans were continually calling on us to surrender. They would broadcast the name of a soldier they had captured and have the soldier say a few words over the radio. Then the Krauts would play American music to try to make us homesick. We loved to listen to this propaganda because we would hear all the latest songs free of charge. Axis Sally, a Nazi radio propagandist with a sexy voice, would supply the music. At least once a week the Germans would shoot over some new leaflets, generally picturing the girl we left behind in the embrace of a fat, old Jewish man. This was known as the "Sam Cohen" series. As soon as we left Anzio, we never saw any more drawings or heard from them again. We had won the battle.

All my Love,
Bob

By May 27, 1944, the German defenses around Cisterna had crumbled. Our company moved toward Artena and Rome.

Dear Folks,

I have a rather funny story to tell you that happened to me early one morning at Artena on our drive toward Rome. However, at the time it wasn't the least bit funny.

Our squad was getting into position for another major attack. We moved along a narrow, slippery trail toward a big gully. As we were going forward, I slipped and took a nasty fall down the rocky side of the ravine. I jarred myself pretty bad and couldn't move. Eventually, squad members succeeded in carrying me out of the gully. By that time we didn't know where our company was located. It was too late to search for them because an artillery barrage was just starting to saturate the area, and we had to hug the ground. Finally, we ran across a major from our battalion who told us to cross about 250 yards of open terrain, and we would find K Company in the woods. The dawn was just breaking as the 5 of us started across the open field. Our artillery was landing in the woods, but we thought nothing of it; our only wish was to cross the field as fast as possible and locate our "missing" platoon. (Naturally, we were not missing; we knew where we were located. The problem was our platoon.)

Just as we were about 50 yards from the woods, two machine guns opened up on our left flank approximately 200 yards away. German tracers sang by directly in front of our faces as well as between us. The Krauts couldn't miss us, but miraculously they did! As I hit the ground, I looked sideways and saw dirt kicking up right along side my body. The bullets were digging in the dirt not more than 2 inches away, but we were all untouched. Of course, we realized our company was not in the woods, but the Jerries were there. It was impossible to remain in the open field. We were sitting ducks. In a matter of minutes the Germans would have adjusted their range and finished us off. We made up our minds mighty fast, and the next thing you knew we were dashing straight towards the woods that held the Germans. At least we were safe for the moment from that blistering machine-gun fire. The Krauts must have thought we were nuts; they scattered. By the time we caught our breath and looked around, there were no Germans to be seen. However, our artillery was falling dangerously close. Once again we wondered what to do. We couldn't push any further into the woods because we would most definitely run into trouble from the Krauts. If we returned, we'd be cut down by bullets either from our own troops or the Germans. We had only one choice; we stood our ground and waited for our main attack to commence.

We could see our boys begin to work their way out of the gully and move toward us. They looked mighty good until they started shooting into the woods where we were hiding. We stayed low and hoped they wouldn't think we were Jerries. It would be tough to be killed by our own men. We gave a big sigh of relief when we "surrendered" to our men and eventually rejoined K company. As for the major who misdirected us, we never saw him again.

With Love to the "Mighty Bunch,"
Bob

I must mention that during those days following the breakthrough, there were episodes where our tanks unknowingly fired on their own men, where our artillery shells fell among us, and where our Allied planes bombed and strafed us. It was unfortunate, but it did happen. Casualties did result from such mistakes.

The breakthrough produced enough horrible bloody sights to last me for all eternity. I can never obliterate the wrenching sight of so many young men brutally mutilated or gasping for their last breath. I could not help them, but we must not forget them. They cannot have died in vain. Their memories must be preserved forever.

Dear Willie,

School must be nearly over by now. Are you going to pass everything? How is math coming? You'll probably be the first to go swimming this year; so please tell me how cold the water is when you stick your toes in. Mine are still freezing from Anzio; trenchfoot is rampant. By next year, I hope to be home swimming with everyone.

I hear you have been making airplane models. Made any good ones? They tell me you have a hard time trying to find enough dough to go to the movies and buy models. The movie prices seem awfully high. Tell you what I'll do; I'll give you $5 and you take the whole family to the movies some night and get some ice cream after the picture. Get Mimi to take the five dollars out of my monthly check, and you can surprise them. Ok by you? Bye now.

"Money-bags" Bob

On June 4, 1944, our reconnaissance patrols reached Rome. Two days later the Allies landed in Normandy; Italy became second-rate news; Rome was secured. It was interesting to note that the crowds were absent as we entered Rome; most kept to themselves behind locked doors.

The fields of Anzio were saturated with thousands and thousands of mines. I wonder how many Italians were killed or mutilated after the war when hitting or stepping on a "lost" mine.

To this day the Anzio campaign continues to fuel bitter controversy. Following successful landings, why did we (the Allies) fail to aggressively press forward as formulated by our original strategy and capture Rome? The finger appears to point toward generalship. Was this campaign one of the greatest military blunders in World War II? The debate continues.

June 7, 1944

Dear Folks,

Today the long-awaited news hit us—The Allies have invaded France! It may sound wonderful, but I know what those poor GIs are going through. I hope those Jerries hurry up and throw in the towel.

Love,
Bob

Rome
June 1944

Dear Willie,

I think you're going to be surprised when I tell you I found an amusement area in Rome. It's only a little one with a roller coaster, whip, merry-go-round, ferris wheel, shooting gallery and other so-called "Gus Games." [Note: Playland in Rye, NY, had an amusement park. An individual by the name of Gus owned most of the "games of chance."] The roller coaster costs 5 lire (5 cents) to ride while the ferris wheel is 2 lire and the shooting gallery 10 lire. (I can shoot Germans for free so why pay 10 lire.)

I visited the catacombs; the Italian sales team was out in full force selling all sorts of religious articles to the soldiers. Trolleys take you to various parts of the town, but it's easy to get lost. Although I have a map of Rome I still lost my way. There is plenty to drink; nothing to eat. A bar or two can be found on every street; you name the concoction you want and they will mix it for you.

I'll have to wait until I return home to get a nice juicy steak with potatoes. Speaking of potatoes, I had some real ones a while back. We boiled them in our canteen cups and ate them as fast as we could. The second time we baked the potatoes in the coals of the bonfire. I doubt if I'll be able to get anymore spuds for another 6 months or so. I had two more treats that I'll tell you about. One night we "found" several chickens running about. In the twinkling of an eye, these "lost chicks" had lost their heads. The pot was put on the fire, and the food prepared for boiling. At two o'clock in the morning we had a grand meal of chicken under fire. You can't imagine how good they tasted!

Another time, we passed a dairy farm with plenty of well-fed cows. Everyone had loads of nice, sweet, warm milk to drink; I had a canteen cup full which I changed into chocolate milk by mixing cocoa with the milk. We get the cocoa from our C rations in case you had forgotten.

Our PX rations came through about a week or two ago. I had some Hershey bars and Butterfingers. As an added treat, we had 1/2 a bottle of Coca-cola to guzzle. That's the first time I've had any coke since leaving the States a long time ago.

Love to All,
Bob

Rome: It's Great to Be Alive

The most important piece of information we received as we entered Rome came from Fifth Army Headquarters. It read "3rd Infantry Division Will Garrison Rome!" This news was beyond belief to members of the battle-weary 3rd. It meant the war was over for us. The days of living in hell were past. We could look to the future with hope in our eyes.

June 9, 1944
Dear Folks,

I seem to have more trouble keeping a watch than any twenty soldiers. I just broke another one that had been bestowed upon me by a captured German soldier. The pocket watch now looks like a piece of mangled metal. The first sign of trouble popped up when the inner spring broke followed by the crystal and hour-hand coming loose. The final chapter occurred when I fell and dented the back somehow.

The news of the Halsted Place fire has just reached me. Are the renters still living there? It's awfully fortunate that you had fire insurance on the house. I trust you will be reimbursed sufficiently so that you can complete the necessary repairs.

Guess it's time to say goodnight. Hope everything turns out okay.

Bob

June 12, 1944

Dear Civilians,

You are not "stealing a march" on me by having all the warm weather. It is extremely warm around those parts too. I must admit I sweat a lot wearing O.D.s (olive drab uniforms which are generally worn in the winter months). We wear O.D.s at all times of the year (morning, noon and night).

We are starting to notice a few stray fresh fruits appear on our daily menu. I could eat fruit until it comes out of my ears. It is funny but when I could have all the fruit I wanted in the states I didn't eat too many varieties. However, now I try to get all the fruit I can. I've even eaten fresh apricots and liked them, but I still don't do handstands for the canned apricots. Time to hurry now. Gotta go pickin'. Bye!

Love to All,
Bob

June 14, 1944

Dear Folks,

The censors tell us we are permitted to say we have visited the City of Rome. I know what Daddy will ask me; so I'll tell him that I've seen the top cathedrals in the world. Some of these huge churches would take your breath away. Our church in Rye would fit in one of their side altars. The paintings on the walls are something you read about in books but never expect to see. They are really beautiful! The ceilings seem to touch the heavens.

I received some fudge in one of your packages along with a pocket knife. It's certainly a swell one. Thanks loads for sending it. The other day I received a letter from Ann's sister, Joan. Sometime ago she asked me what I thought about the soldier-vote question. Her history teacher wanted to know what the fellows overseas thought on this subject; so I wrote and told her. The teacher read my letter to the history class; they thought my reply was excellent.

Love to All "Twenty-Three,"
Bob

Once in Rome the 3rd Infantry Division quickly established guard posts throughout the "Eternal City" in order to prevent sabotage by the fascists to Rome's major power and communications centers. During our first few days my outlook on life took a 180-degree turn. Rome was a great city to sightsee. In general, the people were pleasant. The girls were gorgeous, and life was pretty good after all. I felt good to be alive. Now I could breathe freely again and my guardian angel could take a spiritual respite. We both needed it.

The American soldiers in Rome who were of Italian ancestry or spoke some Italian were in great demand. Those who did not fall into either category quickly learned the value of cigarettes, gum, or chocolate when bartering with a "damsel in distress".

June 21, 1944

Dear Daddy,

I'm writing to you today because I would like to tell you a little more about some of the cathedrals and churches I've visited. I went to the dome of St. Peters and from there the whole city stretches before you. Once you visit the Vatican you'll never forget it, although it's hard to describe the true beauty of this city. I've sent some postcards home of the cathedral. You can get a better idea of the Vatican from these photographs.

Another memorable church is the Church of Santa Maria degli Angeli. I have a clipping from our newspaper, the *Stars and Stripes*, about the Mass of Thanksgiving which was attended by nearly 10,000 Allied troops last week. I was there at the Mass; it was breathtaking.

While visiting Rome I was lucky enough to be present at Irving Berlin's *This Is the Army*. Berlin sang "Oh, How I Hate to Get Up in the Morning, White Christmas, Alexander's Ragtime Band" and two of his latest hits, "There Are No Wings in a Foxhole" and "The Fifth Army's Where My Heart Is." Ever hear of them? The show was presented in Rome's huge opera house. It had an all-soldier cast. The music and everything was great. Before I close, I want to give Willie these stamps. This is the end of the Italian collection. I have a couple of German ones that I will "dig up."

Love to All,
Bob

June 19, 1944

Dear Folks,

Your garden undoubtedly is out in full bloom. I wish we could be planting the garden together, but I guess not this year. The Christmas box of Fanny Farmer candy just arrived. Took quite a long time, didn't it? (I suppose Santa is getting old or he missed my new street address.)

July 2, 1944

Dear Auntie,

After not having any "shots" since leaving for Anzio, I got hit twice the other day. I certainly seem to have received my share of shots.

Well, the year is half over and things look a hundred percent better. Russia is rolling along nicely. Let's hope the Germans crack soon. Whatever happens I trust we show the Germans no mercy. If I had my way, I'd crush them all.

I had a laugh at the Republican Party's recent platform. In our paper it said one of their aims was "to get our boys home from overseas." Now isn't that a silly policy statement. No one can return until the war is over, and then one will have to await his turn. Eventually, we'll come back, won't we?

July 7, 1944

Dear Folks,

Daddy remarked how uninterested a fellow was in a *Life* magazine picture when a shell landed nearby. Don't think this is too uncommon for it's not. Many times I have had shells go off mighty close, and I just keep on going as if nothing happened. Of course, sometimes the shell explodes before you hear it, but the majority of the times you hit the ground and let the shrapnel fly over your head.

I'm going to make this letter short so I can enclose the newspaper article I read about the government offering to send veterans back to school. I don't know if I'll ever return to N.Y.U. I've forgotten too much to start my senior year. Also, it's going to be hard to return to the books and study after 2 years of killing. It depends a lot on when I get discharged from the army. I won't even think about it until I get back to the States. That will be soon enough for me.

I noticed in your letter that I had a card to mail back in order to vote. Maybe I'm stupid but I am not going to return it. To me whoever wins the presidency is a minor question. There are many more important things I have to do and worry about than sending in my vote. Incidentally, I feel Dewey is 4 years too early.

July 8, 1944

Dear "Twenty-Three,"

I received a letter from my pal in Illinois, Russell Law, today. Where do you think he is? Right! He's back in Illinois at the Mayo General Hospital. That's one of the best hospitals in the land. He told me he had hoped to visit you when he passed through New York, but he couldn't make it. Isn't that too bad? It would have been wonderful if he could have come to Rye and visited everyone. He was always going to come to Rye with me, but I don't know now.

My paycheck dropped by recently, but I didn't send any money home. The previous month I spent all my pay in Rome. I only had a partial pay that month; now I have received all my back pay. We have not as yet seen the extra $10 a month combat pay. Guess we will eventually; hope it's before the war is over.

Although my letters home were quite cheerful in June and July 1944, my inner emotions were being churned up. I felt the weight of the world was on my shoulders. By mid-June we had been informed that the 3rd Infantry Division would be shortly invading southern France. Another first-wave amphibious landing! One was enough for any soldier, but two. . . . That would be really stretching my luck.

Prior to the end of June I was in my new bivouac area and undergoing intensive amphibious training. From my letters to the states I could not give the slightest hint of what was transpiring. All that my friends and folks knew was that I was safe and not engaged in actual combat.

July 15, 1944

Dear Folks,

I understand the President finally signed the combat bill. That means an extra $10 monthly in our pockets. I imagine the pay increase will be included in this month's check. [Wonder why it took so long for this bill to materialize? The war started December 7, 1941; here it is 2 1/2 years later.]

I know you like to receive regular letters from me, but it is often impossible to send anything other than V-mails. (Combat conditions.) Whenever I can, I will always send a pen 'n' ink letter with V-mails in-between.

Love to All,
Bob

July 19, 1944

Dear Folks,

Ann sent a lovely picture of herself framed in a green leather case which easily fits in my pocket. Speaking of pictures, where the devil are yours? You mentioned you would send some several months ago, but, I guess, the sun hasn't been out. You'd better have them taken pretty soon. This is my final warning. At this rate I won't be able to recognize anyone when I return to Rye.

I'll be very happy to receive the *Rye Chronicle* newspaper every week. That's a great idea because I enjoy reading what's going on back home.

The element of surprise for our pending daytime assault against the Germans on the Riviera was greatly diminished when the 3rd Infantry Division conducted a practice landing on the beaches outside Naples in broad daylight before hundreds of Italians. (I'm sure they took notes.) Another factor was the tremendous increase in ship concentration of all types in Naples harbor. These circumstances prompted the Germans to erect new underwater obstacles along the French beaches. At this time the Naples area was over-run with pro-Nazis and fascists.

The dog days of July seemed to quickly slip by. Our training program neared an end; graduation day was approaching.

July 29, 1944

Dear Folks,

I have not been able to write you in nearly a week; so I'm going to scribble you this V-mail mighty quick.

I understand that Russell had a 17-day leave from the hospital. His mother says he's not as nervous anymore, but she doubts if he will ever be able to raise his arm again. It was his right arm too. He gets a 3 day pass once a month. I wrote Mrs. Law after I received her letter and thanked her for everything.

Dear Folks,

It's funny but while I've been in the military I have never broken any bones. If some of the things ever happened to me in civilian life that occurred in the Army, I would be in the hospital every 6 months. While practicing for our assault landing in France, we had a compass problem one night during which we had to cross a mountain range. It was pitch black, and we were getting nowhere. I became extremely impatient at our lack of progress, grabbed the compass, and told the squad to follow me. I took 5 steps and disappeared off a high cliff. As I hurled down, I remember kicking my feet in mid-air and tumbling all around. I struck the ground full force, landing on my rear end. A couple of seconds later my helmet caught up with me. Wham! It clipped me on the arm. I thought every bone in my body was broken. With help I hobbled back to our tent; by morning, I was so stiff, I could hardly move. No more training for me. Gradually, all the aches 'n' pains and black 'n' blue marks disappeared. However, I can still recall the terrifying sensation in my stomach as I stepped off into space. I never thought I was going to hit bottom, but I did! It was mighty hard. Nothing gave except me.

Love to All,
Bob

CHAPTER 7

Southern France

3rd Infantry Division Timetable in Southern France

Date	Description
1944	
Jun 13	3rd Infantry Division was notified they would commence amphibious landing training for Southern France invasion.
Aug 8	Final loading aboard ships completed.
Aug 15	D-Day, St. Tropez, France. Awarded French Croix de Guerre.
Aug 15–Sept 14	Race through Southern France—30 DAYS.

Not Again

Our Southern France practice ("dress-rehearsal") landing was under the direct supervision of the U.S. Navy. Although the seas off the port of Naples were choppy, there was no fiasco like in Anzio. During rehearsal we disembarked without any major problems. Let's face it; we were ready! Bring on the Krauts.

It was impossible to hide from the Germans our preparation to invade Southern France. There would be no deception. In fact the Germans kept broadcasting the news that the American troops were preparing to invade Southern France. We, the assault troops, didn't have the slightest idea where the final landing would take place. I can assure you nothing in life is more terrifying than being on a first-wave amphibious landing craft heading directly into the enemy's line of fire, being literally dropped into the dragon's mouth with no place to hide, and expected to wade through waist-deep water while the bullets whistled around you (like sitting ducks). You never knew what lay before you other than almost certain death or injury. We were all alone; no one could come to our aid. One assault landing (Anzio) was enough to last me a lifetime. When we were advised that the 3rd Infantry Division, 15th Regiment, would be shortly making an assault somewhere on the coast of Southern France, my heart skipped a beat or two or more. Here we go again! Old memories and fears flashed before me as I boarded the LCT (Landing Craft Transport). Could I make it through safely a second time? You bet; I was invincible! Besides, my guardian angel was still watching over me. "Arrivederci Roma!"

Note: Winston S. Churchill, Prime Minister of England, was in Italy in early August 1944 and witnessed the Allied Forces departing for the invasion of Southern France.

Southern France, D-Day II
First-Wave Assault: August 15, 1944

A little after 8:00 a.m.,

the ramp of our landing craft dropped down and the 3rd Division swarmed ashore on the beach at St. Tropez, France. As we approached the mainland, we crouched low in the boat so the enemy couldn't tell how many there were of us and also couldn't hit us as easy. The boats were constructed of wood except the hulls and steel ramp in the bow. A bullet would go right through these crafts without any trouble. Approaching the beach we had to be on the alert for our own Navy's rockets. Several fell short and landed dangerously close to our boats. So many rockets went off at once that some were bound to miss their target. As we neared the shore, quite a few exploded in the water around us. Water would gush up like a geyser and spray all over the boat. We would glance up and see another one coming. At the last moment, it seemed as if the rocket would veer slightly and just miss our craft.

Destroyers roamed close to shore and fired their guns at any target that presented itself. If a German gun emplacement cut loose, these destroyers would come in and blast them to pieces. They also laid down smoke screens for the cruisers and battleships that were in our convoy. Far to our right, I watched one of those huge, new battlewagons go into action. They really would emit a tremendous blast! Fire would belch out; the ship would rock, and you'd hear a terrible roar. It was certainly a sight to behold.

Minutes before we hit land, a machine-gun sprayed the water around us. We prayed and waited until the landing craft had ground over the sand. Southern France had been invaded! When the ramp came down, we scrambled to get out as fast and as orderly as possible. It was much safer on the beach. As soon as we were unloaded, the Navy sailor would back the craft out and head to a larger boat which was far enough away to be out of range of any shore guns. Next group were waiting.

Although hard to believe, the beach was practically deserted; resistance was scattered. In less than an hour K Company had seized their initial objective, completely reorganized, and moved inland to their next objective. These positions, likewise, were lightly manned by the Germans and quickly overrun. Casualties were minimal.

I never told you about the grand meals we had on our U.S. ship while practicing our landing in Southern France. I worked KP and ate cakes, pies and cookies. "A little bit of heaven," I used to say. For breakfast I often had fresh fruit such as apples and oranges. Of course, I had some kind of meat for lunch and supper. To top the day off the Navy sold ice cream at night; the KPs and sailors were served first. Not bad, eh? I know darn well I should have joined the Navy instead of enlisting in the Army. There were movies later on in the evening. I saw *This Is the Army*.

The Race for Freedom

During the first few days after our landing, I was introduced to many well-organized French resistance groups. My high school and college French came in handy as town after town quickly fell to our division. Tanks and tank destroyers were used with the infantry to patrol and clear roads. It was a common sight for an entire rifle battalion to move down the road atop tanks and trucks. The French resistance groups often seized towns and held them until our arrival. Regiment movement by truck became more commonplace; reconnaissance patrols were seen 15–20 miles in front of our regiment. Sabotage activities became prevalent. Small arms firefights were common. Most rear-guard positions consisted of small German detachments that eventually withdrew. Our rapid advance did present many supply problems.

August 23, 1944

Dear Gang,

Were you looking for a letter from me? Well, here it is direct from France. Naturally, you must have surmised I was involved in the landing when you heard Southern France was invaded. I was right there in the front row, reserved section. I couldn't miss it, could I? Nothing unusual.

This is the first V-mail I've written; so I'll tell you as much as I can. Right now I wish I could remember all the French I learned in high school. I can understand a little what the French say but not too much. Perhaps it'll come back to me in due time.

The French people treat us great as we liberate their villages. Everyone pours into the streets, yelling, clapping, dancing, laughing, and hugging as we go by. They offer you all the wine you can guzzle and all the melons you can eat. There is a warm feeling of friendship throughout the countryside. The people realize what a wonderful gift freedom is.

"Au Revoir,"
Bob

August 29, 1944

Dear Folks,

Yesterday we had our first mail call in France, and I received loads of letters. I'm afraid you will have to do my writing for me for a while. (I'm too busy.) Try and thank Chickie, Alice Sloat, Bob Thornton, Gene White and Russell Law for their swell letters.

In town after town we chased the Jerries out, and the people went nuts over us. I ate peaches as big as apples and lovely, juicy pears and melons. In one village, someone brought out a bugle and everyone joined in song. You should have heard the French voices ring out when he played the French National Anthem. Golly! Everyone both young and old sang with all their heart and soul. Later on we played "The Star Spangled Banner," and the American soldiers showed the French that we too were proud of our country.

There is no need to tell you of the grand job the French underground is doing; you've read about it in the papers. They are a major factor for our success in Southern France.

All my Love,
Bob

Instead of hiking, we sped by truck through the French countryside. Everywhere you looked the roads were littered with burned out cars, tanks, halftracks, and dead Germans. Our artillery had caught the

Germans trying to escape and had annihilated them. Prisoners came in by the hundreds. The fleeing Nazis discarded tons of German equipment.

Let's Hope the Auto Club Can Help!

September 7, 1944

Dear Folks,

I had some fried eggs the other day from some French people. They were delicious! The French have only brown eggs, but they are not too bad. Sometimes, we trade our C rations for eggs and bread. Whenever a town in France is liberated, you can hear the church bells start to ring. Even if you are many miles away, you would hear the bells and know the Germans had flown northward, leaving the village undefended. Today we captured over 100 Germans in one town alone and wounded just as many. What a nice haul! (For us!)

Generally, it's hard to talk about oneself. My report card on my military career would be full of ups and downs. As I look back, there were occasions where one might label me a "clown," especially when I was playing tricks on my own buddies or lieutenant.

I recall many days in Southern France when the enemy was invisible; they had pulled the bulk of their troops northward, leaving town after town unguarded. During this period, I was handling a light machine gun. My buddy and I would trade off carrying the gun vs. ammunition. The ammunition was contained in a compact but rather deep metal box. Our food rations were boring to put it mildly. Bearing in mind the situation plus the fact there were no Germans to our knowledge in the immediate vicinity, it should come as no surprise that when our squad came upon a field of potatoes ready for plucking, I decided to dump the ammo for a peck of potatoes. I figured at night I could easily cook up potatoes for everyone and also replenish my ammunition. Good thinking! The bullets were dumped and the potatoes inserted. Everything was progressing nicely until a cry for a machine gunner up front was heard. Now, what did I do? I was not in the lieutenant's good graces because of past "tricks," so he would not be too happy with my latest caper. Up we went with our machine gun and ammunition (aka potatoes). The lieutenant instructed us to set up the gun and commence firing at the Krauts in the distance. My buddy placed the gun in position. He was ready; I was not. Sheepishly, I explained the "Case of the Missing Bullets" as laughter permeated the air. I was in deep trouble for the umpteenth time. According to the lieutenant, my punishment was to be a court-martial! For this military offense I calculated that my worst sentence would be a transfer to another infantry company. What difference would it make to me? None, truthfully.

Eventually, cooler heads prevailed and in time the matter faded away, but my name did not fade in the lieutenant's mind. I would always be an "acting squad leader"; the actual promotion to sergeant would never come.

In our daily news bulletin, I see we are permitted to mention some places where we've fought. Since there isn't too much news we can write about, due to censorship, I may as well enlighten you a mite. The fighting is extremely light at present; the German divisions are widely dispersed. From the souvenir copy of our newspaper which I sent, you can get an idea of the general area where we have been. The only thing is that we came much closer to Marseille than it appears on the map. The first town we hit was St. Tropez, but after that most of the villages were just unknown names. Montelimar was very costly for the German army. Our artillery knocked out 222 vehicles in one day. From Besancon (Southern France), we fought northward to Vesoul (Vosges Mountains) and Lure (perhaps you can find these towns on another map). Anyway we are allowed to mention places we've attacked only up to a certain date; so my letter must stop at St. Ame, a little town past Remiremont.

"C'est tout for today. Viva La France,"
Robert

Dear Auntie,

My teeth are going from bad to worse. I know at least one will have to come out. The rest are full of holes. I had one fixed at Anzio but the filling fell out 5 days later. As far as I am concerned, the Army can junk all dental equipment. The fillings the dentists give you overseas are useless.

The roads continue to be littered with demolished German equipment and dead Krauts. It is a grand sight for U.S. soldiers. I only wish our artillery could do it every day.

Somewhere in France
(30 days since invasion)
September 17, 1944

Dear Folks,

I had a couple of letters from Mrs. Law and Russell recently. It seems that Russell's arm is much better, and he can raise it straight out from his body. He expects to return to college in October, providing his discharge comes through.

Does it get cold here in France! Whew! I hope this war ends before it gets much colder; my feet won't be able to take another freezing like they did last year.

Vosges Mountains
September 21, 1944

Dear Twenty-Three,

At last I have received your letters, and you know I am running around France. While resting several minutes in a little French town, I walked into the local church. The place was constructed in 1899 and was in great condition except on the walls were painted huge German Swastikas. They were plastered all over the church; you couldn't miss them. Incidentally, the Germans wear swastikas belt buckles which translate to "God With Us."

Willie asked me if I had any souvenirs such as German helmets or knives. All that I can say is that there are hundreds of these items around, but I haven't any nor have my buddies. We cannot send souvenirs home at present.

I've gotten my winter undershirt on. It feels good. It was darn cold without it. I don't know when I'll be able to write again. Fighting is extremely intense. There is no rest! The vacation is over.

Dear Chums,

I thought I was going to have my watch ticking again; but the French civilian who tried his talents on the balky subject couldn't do a thing with it. I'm still without a watch that works but it shouldn't be too long before I "discover" one. I almost had a watch the other day, but my pal forgot me. We had just captured 4 Jerries, and I and another fellow went after 2 more. The first Germans captured were searched and a few watches were found and removed from their possession. There was one watch overlooked. Consequently, someone behind the lines "discovered" it. I must admit we did catch the 2 Jerries, and I came up with a great Luger pistol. You see, in combat we grab the pistols and watches. As a result, the capture of the 2 Germans didn't turn out too bad for me after all.

With Love to "Der Gang,"
Bob

October 16, 1944

Dear Folks,

I believe I haven't ever mentioned the French gals to you. The French lassies scamper out when we "liberate" their villages and kiss us "mugs" on the cheeks as we begrudgingly go by. We never stay long in any place. (Darn the luck.)

While I was talking to some of the older French folks, one mentioned the word "timbres," and so I traded some of our U.S. stamps for a couple of French and German ones. I'll stick a few in this envelope for Willie.

I see he has the same French teacher that I had. Does he get 100's in his tests? Since he studies French, I'll relate to him a story about the Germans and French which took place in a local village. It seems that the FFI (Forces Francaise D'Interieure) were fairly active in this particular sector, and the Germans discovered where, they believed, the leader of the French movement lived. The people of the village hid him rather than turn him over to the Boche. In fact, they hung and painted the Cross of Lorraine on their houses in defiance. All this time our division was drawing closer and closer. The Jerries realized they must soon leave, but not before they had taught these "arrogant" French (as the Germans called them) a lesson. And so it was that one dark night these "brave" conquerors set fire to many houses and farms in the village. By the time we entered, the homes had mostly been demolished by fire. Hardly anything remained except the church which stood untouched in the village square. Only charred timbers could be seen, where 2 months before was a picturesque old French town.

War is hell,
Bob

Wreckage of a French Town

Every town had stories to relate of German atrocities. Apparently, the Boche would go wild as we approached. They would strip the towns of all food, ransack and burn the houses, and destroy the farm machinery and crops. Men, women, and children were beaten, tortured, and raped or killed. We were told it was not uncommon for the Germans to line-up the French civilians and slaughter them.

CHAPTER 8

Vosges Mountains to Colmar

3rd Infantry Division Timetable in Vosges Mountains and Colmar Pocket

Date	Description
1944	
Sept 15	Winter campaign commences. 3rd Infantry Division enters the Vosges Mountains without any significant combat interruption since St. Tropez invasion on August 15, 1944.
Sept 30	Heavy forest fighting; increased German artillery fire as division pushes through Vagney, St. Ame, and Le Tholy.
Oct 2	Devotion to "the Guardian Angels." (A special day of remembrance.)
Oct 20	Division reaches Meurthe River. Casualties mount as tree-bursts of artillery and mortar shells take heavy toll.
Nov 1–Nov 5	Le Haut Jacques—bloody, intense uphill fighting (worse than Anzio). To advance a few hundred yards took five days.
Nov 10–Nov 18	River-crossing training commences on Meurthe River. Numerous reconnaissance patrols cross icy river at night to gather German troop data and return.
Nov 19–Nov 20	Meurthe River crossed by 3rd Infantry Division via temporary footbridges.
Nov 22–Nov 23	German Winter Line penetrated (Saales).
Nov 24–Nov 30	German Winter Line destroyed. Advance toward Strasbourg and Rhine River. Numerous prisoners taken; extreme number of enemy casualties. Continuous sniper, street, and hand-to-hand fighting. Brutal artillery fire from both sides.
Nov 26–Nov 27	French enter Strasbourg.
Dec 1	3rd Infantry Division takes up defensive positions on the outskirts of Strasbourg. Guns trained on Reich.

Date	Description
1944	
Dec 2	Various units of 3rd Infantry Division relieved and sent to rest areas for several days.
Dec 13	3rd Infantry Division moves into sector previously held by 36th Infantry Division; prepares to eliminate Colmar Pocket (south of Strasbourg).
Dec 23–Dec 29	Extremely savage fighting for six days northeast of Colmar. Merry Christmas.
Dec 31	I was transferred from light machine-gunner to light mortar.
1945	
Jan 22	Final all-out attack to eliminate Colmar Pocket begins. Hill #216 recaptured by U.S. 254th Infantry.
Jan 30	Colmar Canal breached under brutal conditions (see Presidential Citation).
Feb 7	Neuf-Brisach cleared of German forces. After 188 days of nonstop combat, the 3rd Infantry Division is relieved of frontline duty.
Feb 20	3rd Infantry Division awarded second French Croix de Guerre with Palm "entitling its members to wear coveted fourragere." Only American division to receive this French decoration.
Mar 12	Back to combat.

The Vosges Mountains: Living on the Edge
September 15, 1944–January 21, 1945

By mid-autumn our division was knocking on the door of the Vosges Mountains, one of the cruelest places on the face of the earth. The cold, blistery winds were already whipping across the countryside; the torrential rains were beginning to make their presence felt. Another winter was just around the corner.

Since landing in St. Tropez thirty days ago, we never had a chance to rest and catch our breath. And now we were looking at the formidable Vosges Mountains, which in spots reached 3,000 to 4,000 feet skyward. According to research conducted by our division, no army on the attack had ever completely penetrated the enemy defenses in the Vosges. We were expected to accomplish this feat!

The fighting in the heavily wooded Vosges Mountains was the most vicious of the war. It seemed every minute we were facing nerve-wracking artillery barrages. German mortar and artillery fire could completely destroy a platoon or company of U.S. soldiers within a matter of minutes. One of the most terrifying sounds known to mankind is that of an enemy artillery shell growing louder and louder. One second we thought we were safe, praying and hugging the ground, surrounded by trees; the next split second we would feel the breath of death as the shells hit the trees and their destructive power was unleashed directly upon us. At that split second all hell broke loose; the whole world exploded. Red-hot pieces of shrapnel saturated the area. Bodies were savagely ripped apart. The cry for "medic" was heard again and again. We lay there helpless as our buddies' lives slowly ebbed away. It seemed like an eternity before the shelling stopped, the wounded were cared for, and our prayers were answered.

Battle fatigue became a common disease; the daily cases increased dramatically. There was no end to the furious firefights against heavily defended fortifications. I finally realized I was not invincible after all. It was becoming extremely difficult to keep my spirits up day in and day out. Anzio was brutal but the Vosges campaign was far more savage and terrifying. Slowly, I came to believe I probably would not be returning home. The tone of my letters began to change. Death rained down continuously all around me. I could see the fear in the eyes of my buddies and they in mine. I felt the end for me was near.

No matter how hard I tried I could not erase the screams and cries of the dying. A blanket of death covered the Vosges Mountains and the Colmar Pocket. I could feel it, smell it, taste it, see it, and hear it. I could not escape death; death became a part of me. It would never leave me. I was living in pure hell!

Dear "Ration Warriors,"

Hi everybody! Been looking for a letter from me? What shall we gab about today? I don't know what kind of weather you are having but here in France it's miserable. It's the usual rain, mud, fog, and cold that

I encountered last year in Italy. The driving rain reduces our visibility to practically zero. The more I study the war, I don't see when it will end. These Jerries fight on and on even when they have no chance whatsoever. Snipers appear everywhere along our route. Close-range grenade and hand-to-hand fighting is increasing.

Dear Folks,

I nearly lost my life trying to capture some Jerries recently. It was in the Vosges Mountains when a buddy of mine in our squad spotted some Germans in the bushes. I only saw 3 of them with their hands up; so Travis Mann and I went for them. I was in the lead and Travis was covering me. Four Germans that we couldn't see were lying alongside the path with their rifles fully loaded and ready to take us down. Just as I reached the spot of the ambush, a German machine-gun opened up above us and sent everyone, Germans included, diving for cover. Travis and I hit the ground as the bullets whizzed over our heads. The entire squad of Jerries became frightened and decided to give up rather than fight. We came back with numerous pistols and seven husky Kraut prisoners. (Plus our lives.)

Vesoul, France

Dear Auntie,

As I keep mentioning, the French are delighted whenever we liberate one of their villages. Coming into Vesoul, our company walked into a machine-gun nest. Before we knew it, several of our boys were killed. The French brought their bodies to the entrance of the village church, folded their hands over their chests, and covered their bodies with flowers. All during the day people would come to the church, bow their heads in silent prayer, and walk slowly away with tears running down their cheeks. These people were so heart-broken over the death of these unknown soldiers that sacrificed their lives for them that they would do anything to please us. The mayor told us that the people of Vesoul would never forget this morning when they saw the Americans marching over the hill toward their town.

Love to All,
Bob

The action in the Vosges Mountains became extremely violent, and as a result my letter writing to the "Civilians in Rye" practically came to a halt. Many moons later, I wrote of my (mis)adventures.

Dear Folks,

Now let's skip all this talk and open up my book of experiences. Today, you are going to join me in one of our attacks toward the Meurthe River. It is night time, and we have our packs filled with rations and equipment. The moon hasn't quite come out, and all that you can see as you trudge along are black shapes in front of you as you move silently through the woods. The objective this night is to clear the wooded area across that open field in the distance. There is not supposed to be any enemy in the woods, but you never can tell. Let's check our watches so that when 2235 (10:35 p.m.) is at hand, we can all move out together. All right! Take it easy until it's time to move.

The moon is just coming over the mountains, and everyone is up and ready to go. Our scouts have gone ahead of us; it is time to leave. The attack has begun!

As we start forward a silent prayer forms on the lips of the men, praying that all come safely through.

At the crossroads we stop for a minute and listen. We can't hear anything in the woods to our right; so let's go, we have to be well-dug in before morning.

As every step brings us closer to those ugly looking woods, we begin to wonder if there are any Germans waiting for us. It's too darn quiet. It might be an ambush.

We are entering the woods now and still haven't seen or heard a single sound. If the Krauts are here, all hell will break loose in a few seconds. Perhaps I'd better . . .

Suddenly, the stillness of the night is shattered by the murderous sound of a German machine-gun firing directly in front of me. As I dove for the ditch, the bullets made a pretty pattern on the road behind me. This is it, you say. We have to fight for those woods; so there is no use waiting. Damn those Krauts, anyway!

It doesn't take long. Maybe it's only 5 minutes, but nevertheless it seems like an eternity when you are trying to dodge machine-gun bullets and at the same time get a crack at the Germans with your automatic guns.

As quick as it started, it's all over. The wounded have to be cared for and the dead are left where they have fallen. You've got to push on, on to the next objective. You can't stop and rest although you are dead-tired. The woods must be completely cleared before you can call it a night. Until then, you must keep driving forward. Others will fall along the way, but the objective must be taken at all costs. In tomorrow's communiqué you will read where the men advanced 500 yards to the outskirts of St. Die, but it won't mention the heavy fire-fights we were embroiled in or the misery and pain the soldiers had to endure in order to win that small parcel of land. That information is only known to the men who fought so heroically for the piece of wooded ground.

In case you are interested, the above story concerns the night our platoon and I came swarming down out of the Vosges Mountains and fought our way to the Meurthe River. There is a second chapter to this attack, but I will finish it tomorrow. It concluded with Travis Mann and me being listed as MIA (missing in action) behind enemy lines.

I am sure the good Lord and my guardian angel were with me during these battle-scarred days in the Vosges. However, my confidence in my ability to survive slipped considerably.

Our next attack went from bad to worse to murderous:

It started the night we began our assault on St. Die. After a fierce and deadly gun battle, everything became quiet. Travis Mann dug a deep foxhole and covered it with wood and dirt; I, as usual, lay down on the ground and went to sleep for an hour before guard-duty beckoned. Prior to drifting into dreamland, I kidded Travis about his elegant living quarters, and told him he had wasted his energy building such a masterpiece. "You'll never get your investment out." However the following day, I helped him enlarge his fortress so two could sleep in it at night. This proved to be an excellent decision.

The sun was just setting in the west, and I was about 20 feet from our foxhole when the German artillery barrage started. The first aerial blast split a tree not more than 50 feet to my right, and shrapnel zipped by my ear. More and more air-bursts followed so fast that I had no time to do anything except hit the ground and pray. Shrapnel was buzzing all around, but I could not crawl those last 20 feet to safety. That would have meant sure death. In time the shelling let up for a moment, and I actually dove into the foxhole. A minute later, the shelling started again. All that Travis and I could do was lay on our stomachs and pray harder.

When the barrage finally subsided, there were only 5 of us left unharmed. One fellow was shell-shocked and went out of his mind. One was cut in two by shrapnel, and the other members of our two squads were wounded. Travis and I remained in our foxhole while the remaining 3 soldiers took the wounded back. A short time later the shelling started a third time; our 3 buddies did not return. We stayed in our two-man outpost in no man's land all night and most of the following day. At first it never crossed our minds that K Company had been ordered to withdraw and had left us behind enemy lines. You can imagine our surprise when occasionally we spotted Germans patrolling the area. Our company had withdrawn, and we were all alone in German territory. At all cost we had to play dead and lie still so as not to attract attention.

Our new problem was how to work our way back to our lines and at the same time try not to get shot by our own men or the Germans. Where our regiment was located was anyone's guess, but we had to move on.

The afternoon was void of any German troop movement.

Travis and I gathered our paraphernalia and began slowly retracing our steps. We followed the woods, crossed an open space, and "attacked" a group of vacant farm houses. Luckily, the Jerries were not around; so we easily "conquered" the houses without firing a shot. Fresh from victory we washed up and relaxed for a few hours. How peaceful it was! All our cares seemed to evaporate. We were in Shangri-La.

We remained in the farm houses until dark before heading out. We couldn't see the Germans, and they could not see us. All that we knew was the general location of the Krauts; we had to keep a stride ahead of them. Both Travis and I were confident we could locate the missing K company. Eventually, our prayers were answered, about 3:00 a.m. the next morning, we reported back to duty to our first-sergeant. Everyone was delighted to see us; we spent the remainder of the night describing our unexpected survival problem. How we escaped capture I'll never understand.

I might add that neither Travis nor I notified the War Department that K Company was missing in action during this trying period. However, the Secretary of War did inform my parents that I was missing. (Wishful thinking?)

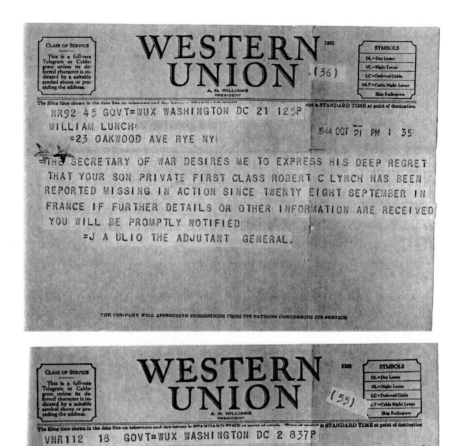

Missing in Action Telegrams

Vosges Mountains

Dear Dad,

I may as well give you the full details on how I was wounded in the leg. Early one morning, our company was situated on a hill overlooking a valley full of Jerries. As our artillery started to land among the enemy, I had a "foolish notion" enter my head to move forward and watch the slaughter by myself. I heard a shell whiz near me; it was too late to hit the ground; I was hit; my leg was bleeding quite profusely.

As you know the pieces of steel from an artillery shell travel so fast you cannot see them. A piece the size of your fingernail could tear off your arm. Shrapnel can cut down almost any size tree. These shells are brutal!

Anyway, I know the good Lord was watching over me that morn because I swear I saw the shrapnel a split second before it hit me. Somehow I moved my leg partially out of its destructive path, resulting in a fairly deep slash and bruise. If I hadn't moved, the leg probably would have been taken off at the knee. It all happened so fast, I didn't realize I was hit until I felt the pain and numbness. Some buddies came and helped me back to the aid station. I could hardly walk. From there a jeep drove by, picked me up, and brought me to battalion medical headquarters where I was patched up. Although I did not have a medical degree, I diagnosed my injury as being healed and released myself. Upon my return to my unit, I was immediately involved in an intense fire-fight with the Jerries. As soon as the battle subsided my lieutenant ordered me to "get the hell out of here" which I did, gladly. For a week or more I barely managed to move about the medical facility. Finally, the wound healed sufficiently to allow me to return to my squad. The leg was fine except when going up hills. I have a scar to remind me of the day I could have lost my leg but was granted the right to keep it thanks to all your prayers. If it wasn't for my foolishness and sticking my neck out all the time, I wouldn't have been wounded. But that's me.

Love to All,
"Pegleg" Bob

November 1944

Dear Fellow-writers,

I have had so many news communiqués concerning Daddy's flashy new bathing suit that I feel it only fitting and proper that I write at least a few lines about it. I suppose he will be going to the beach every week with his tan suit and yellow top. Oh boy! I bet you can spot him a mile away, although who could miss him without the suit. [Dad was quite heavy.] What's this about Daddy putting up the beach umbrella while his trunks kept edging down, lower and lower? Who won? The trunks? I'll have to take his picture when I get home. It'll be a time-exposure shot watching the trunks going into a tail spin. Happy Thanksgiving.

All my Love,
Bob

The Meurthe River was the German Winter Line. Shortly before Thanksgiving, the 7th and 30th Regiments of the 3rd Infantry Division pulled a daring sneak attack; the Meurthe River was breached, the German Winter Line had been broken and their river defenses destroyed. During this period, our 15th Regiment acted as a decoy. Within seven days of the crossing, the 3rd Infantry Division had fought to the gates of Strasbourg and the Rhine River.

Thanksgiving

November 23–28, 1944

Dear Folks,

Our division has set up a rest camp where a certain number of fellows go every few days. Right at this moment, I am at the rest camp catching up on my sleep and calming my nerves. The Army shows movies, and there are showers for the soldiers. Of course, it's only for a few days, but this gives everyone a chance to come and try to relax. No matter how short it may be, it's far better than being up at the front.

I've been paid in full finally, and will be sending you a money order soon for about $120 to put into my bank account. In this payment, we drew our combat pay from last May; so I had an extra $60 coming. From what I understand we are supposed to get the "combat" pay from this past January. Someday I may receive the added $40 owed me.

Love to All,
Bob

Thanksgiving Day

Dear "Twenty-Three,"

Since I am at the rest camp and today (23rd) is Thanksgiving, I expect to have a good meal for dinner. You probably had turkey; so there is no reason why I shouldn't have some too. Boy, will that taste good!

At last I had a haircut; it was so long! You could hardly see my ears before the barber started to cut. There was enough of my hair left over to fill a hair mattress.

I've caught up on my letter writing. I owed about 20 different people but now I'm even until next mail call. You know what I liked in your package of many moons ago? It was the strawberry-apple preserve. Our squad devoured the jam in one night.

This morning (Thanksgiving), I went to the village church where our chaplain said mass. It is interesting to note that the Jerries like to use church steeples for observation posts. As a result, most French church steeples have been destroyed by American artillery.

Saw a funny movie with Gary Cooper and Theresa Wright entitled *Casanova Brown*. See it if you can.

Love,
Bob

November 24, 1944

Dear Gang,

What do you think I had to eat on Thanksgiving Day? We had mashed potatoes, canned corn, turkey, bread 'n' butter, coffee, pie, and cake. Was I full! I finally called it quits. There was plenty of everything; so naturally I had to have an extra piece of pie 'n' cake.

As I was removing my watch, the strap broke. I have my famous watch in my pocket. I am afraid being in my pocket that it can get lost easily. I think I'll store it in my wallet. Need to "capture" another watch as quickly as possible.

Love to All,
Bob

November 26, 1944

Dear "23,"

Thanksgiving Day is over and, I suppose, you've eaten your fill. (And what a fill it must have been.) Tell me confidently, which was stuffed the most—you or the bird. I have my own idea, but I may be wrong.

In one of your recent September letters, you sent me some pictures of everyone. They came out great. I see point rationing has not had much effect on "twenty-three." You couldn't have gained all that weight. I guess the film wasn't put in correctly; that double exposure of Daddy is a wow!

All my Love,
Bob

Dear Auntie,

During these days when the fighting is so intense, we don't get a chance to shave for weeks at a time. You ought to see us. We are wet, tired, and caked with mud and blood. At one time or another, most of us have had moustaches, but I shaved mine off at the first opportunity. I don't like the moustache at all.

Had another letter from Russell. He remembered I broke my wrist watch a long time ago and wanted to send me a new one. Naturally, I wouldn't let him, but it was nice of him to think about it. He always wants to do things for me.

Love to All,
Bob

Maginot Line (France) and Siegfried Line (Germany)

Prior to World War II both France and Germany con-structed/modernized their adjoining frontiers with a system of heavy fortifications. Although the interconnected forts on the Maginot Line presented a complex military problem, the 3rd Infantry Division's offensive strength eventually resulted in both the Maginot and Siegfried lines being breached in the vicinity of Strasbourg.

I wish I could say that when our exhausted company reached Strasbourg our battle assignment was completed. Unfortunately, it did not happen that way. Our division did go on the defensive for a short period of time which gave me the opportunity to rest, lick my wounds, and visit Strasbourg.

Strasbourg

Dear Folks,

I have a couple of postcards of the Cathedral of Strasbourg that I'd like to show you. I was extremely fortunate to attend mass in early December at the Cathedral on the Feast of the Immaculate Conception. The war did not bypass this beautiful church. In fact, most of the win-dows are gone. The people of Strasbourg tell us the Cathedral was hit three times by bombs, but the damage is not too great. The clock, which is world-famous, had been removed and stored underground. I did not see the clock but did see everything else. The face of the Cathedral is a real masterpiece.

As I mentioned, the French forces captured the City of Strasbourg. Our 15th Regiment occupied positions south of the city along the

Rhine River; the 3rd Division began its famous "Watch on the Rhine." (We watched the Germans as well as for the coming of Santa.)

Hope you have a great Christmas. I'll be home next year to help you celebrate.

Bob

December 1, 1944

Dear Folks,

At our last village I met some young French boys (age 7 and 4). Since I had loads of candy, I gave them 2 whole boxes for Christmas. Boy, were they happy! One little fellow hadn't ever seen chocolate. (The war was on when he was born.) He ate it ever so slowly and thought it was wonderful. The Germans wouldn't allow the French parents to teach their children anything but German; so now the children have to learn French and forget their German. By the time we left, the little four year old lad had picked up some of our slang such as "okay and okay-doak." We had our pictures taken with the family. I wrote Ann and Russell and thanked them for their Christmas remembrances. Eventually, I hope to write everyone, but things look pretty hopeless at present. The fighting has been very ferocious, artillery fire never ceases, tree bursts are incessant! Survival is no longer on a day to day basis but minute to minute.

Love to All,
Bob

December 2, 1944

Dear Folks,

One of the fellows asked our mail orderly if we could send some Nazi flags and stuff home. He said it would be fine. The only trouble is that back at the base censorship sector, the fellows have the bad habit of "borrowing" some of our souvenirs. I'll take a chance and mail everything to you. I don't want to carry the stuff around with me; so homeward bound it goes. I've got about everything from soup to nuts; some of it should reach you safely. The main things are the Nazi flags and German arm band. The rest includes a couple of German medals and ribbons. No German bodies, though.

Santa Claus will be coming shortly; so you may as well use $25 and buy some presents. While you're at it, will you find a little something for Ann? I'm stuck here and can't get out to buy anything this year.

Merry Christmas!
Bob

December 4, 1944
Dear Folks,

I hate to talk about combat, but I have a fairly funny story connected with the Jerries. One day we were moving through densely wooded areas, attempting to capture the high ground around us. One American soldier behind me saw some soldiers up the trail in front of us. He thought they were Americans waving "hello"; so he waved back. As we came closer, we saw that they were not waving "hello" but were Germans trying to give up.

At the time I was carrying a carbine. This gun held a clip of bullets. There were 2 buttons on the rifle—one a clip (bullet) release and right next to it a safety catch. As I approached the Jerries, I realized my safety clip was on. Not too bright when you are trying to capture the enemy. However, I knew the Jerries had no way of knowing whether or not my safety was on. (Could not discharge my carbine.) Without missing a beat I slowly slipped my hand around the clip and released the safety, or so I thought. At that moment, the clip of bullets was released from the gun (I had pressed the wrong button), and all my ammunition tumbled to the ground. Now I had an empty gun to capture armed Krauts. The odds did not appear to be in my favor. It was one of those days, I thought. Don't give up yet.

I was careful not to exhibit any surprise when the clip was released but kept walking forward toward the Germans, waving my gun and yelling "Achtung! cummon zee here." Fortunately for me, they did not open fire but meekly surrendered. Thank goodness.

Love to All—Enjoy the holidays,
Bob

Dear Folks,

This time I am going to relate a story that involved our artillery as well as our infantrymen, but before I go into the details, I want to explain that even the best of plans can go horribly wrong in war. Our General McNair was inadvertently killed by U.S. bombers. It is so hard in battle to pinpoint the infantry's whereabouts accurately that lots of accidents occur. The story I am about to relate is one of those.

It was 6:20 exactly and our attack was about to begin. Our objective was a French town about six kilometers away. Just before entering the town our artillery was ordered to fire a tremendous barrage into the village and level it. As we were walking along on the outskirts of the town, we heard our artillery guns start booming in the distance. The seconds ticked by, and we could hear the shells getting closer, and closer, and

CLOSER! Just up the road a mite, a shell landed. Instead of reaching the town the shells were hitting all around us. Shell after shell was poured upon the road where we were crouched. Suddenly, the road blew up in front of me. My God! The shrapnel was cutting us to ribbons; there was no place to hide. We had to lay unprotected on the ground. Every time a shell landed close by, you would steel yourself for the shrapnel that was sure to hit you. It was hellish laying there and expecting to be wounded at any moment. You could hear the screams of the wounded and dying. I saw one of my buddies crawl into the bushes leaving a trail of blood behind him. He died in those thick bushes. When it was over, our nerves were so shaken that we fired at any little sound. One wounded fellow was walking back with 2 soldiers helping him. A shell had exploded close to him, and he had lost his eyesight.

Inside the town there was a shell hole right in the center of the road. On either side lay 2 dead soldiers. Both had been killed by concussion. There wasn't another mark on them. To add to the irony of the story, there was not a Jerry within 10 miles. The casualties from our own artillery were higher than they would have been if we had engaged the enemy for days in a savage fire fight.

In today's wonderful age of technology this unfortunate error could have been corrected in a matter of minutes and casualties probably would not have materialized. However, in 1944, the armies of the world were not blessed with a communication system that is available to the 21st century service men. Field phones did not always work. Let me present the communication problem in World War II from a different perspective. Communications were so antiquated in WWII that today it would be like sending up smoke signals to warn the settlers (soldiers) of a pending attack.

Dear Folks,

Auntie once wrote and asked where I slept at nights. I don't know exactly where to begin, but I'll try to "enlighten" you.

Many times we have daylight objectives to capture. As soon as the area has been cleared of Germans, we dig our foxholes (I am not the greatest digger) and sleep in them. There is always guard duty around our perimeter and night patrols behind enemy lines to be undertaken; so you don't get too much sleep. Early in the morning, you are on the attack again. Often the terrain is not suitable for a daylight assault. Instead of sleeping you shove off in an all-night attack. At the break of day you, hopefully, complete the capture of your objective and try to get in a wink or two. Sleep does not come easy nor often.

There are numerous times lately when you have the opportunity to sleep in a deserted house after pulling guard duty. Italy was rough; you seldom were in a house. However, in France and Germany we have been fortunate to catch a nap under a roof instead of outside in the pouring rain in a foxhole.

As I understand the situation back home, food is becoming harder and harder to come by. Rationing! More and more people will be starting victory gardens this year. I know you have a great vegetable and flower garden. Save some carrots for me.

All my Love,
Bob

I've never run into such harsh weather as descended on us in the Vosges Mountains. Santa would never find us. On a "hot" day the high might have reached minus 10 degrees; at night the bottom dropped out. Think what that meant to the soldier fighting to stay alive.

December 17, 1944

Dear Folks,

I wouldn't have the slightest use for a sleeveless sweater. If you haven't already sent it, you may as well give it to Willie. Perhaps he would wear it.

It's funny but I never know what day of the week it is until I write my letters. Every day is just like the other, and no one cares whether or not it is the seventh or tenth day.

There is no use writing any more today; there is nothing positive to dwell upon. Death is all around; the fighting is fierce and the casualties are staggering.

My nerves are shot.

Love to All;
Enjoy Christmas!
Bah Humbug

Next Assignment: The Colmar Pocket—
17 Terrifying Days

To the south of Strasbourg approximately 30,000 Germans were firmly entrenched in a pocket that was dubbed the "Colmar Pocket." The Germans had to be eliminated in order to secure Strasbourg and the entire Alsace region. The Seventh Army, of which the 3rd Infantry Division was an integral part, quickly recognized that a "full-scale coordinated army-size attack was going to be required to eliminate the Germans."

The 3rd Infantry Division was ordered to relieve the 36th Infantry Division on December 13, 1944 and remove the "Pocket." What followed on December 23 was the start of some of the most savage, violent battles in the entire war. The official records of the 3rd Infantry Division stated that Colmar was "an area whose elimination was to develop into our second greatest fight of the war. Some said the greatest, as in the same degree of ferocity as the attack to break the Anzio "iron-ring"!

Christmas Time 1944

As the holidays approached the German high command announced they would retake Strasbourg as a "Christmas present for der Fuhrer." For six days (December 23–29) our company was involved in an intense struggle for survival with some of Germany's most fanatic, well-disciplined, and intelligent soldiers. Vicious firefights lasted all day and night; mortar and artillery fire was so furious on both sides that the wounded could not be attended to immediately. The captured and wounded soon reached astronomical numbers. Death covered the entire region. Wherever we looked, we saw the torn bodies of our buddies. I kept thinking no one would ever survive the ferocity of these enemy counter-attacks.

> I suppose you would like to hear about my "merry" Christmas. Unknowingly, you have probably read about our exploits in the newspapers. During this period, the frenzied Germans reverted to "suicidal" house-to-house fighting which continued for days without letup. We brought flame throwers into the battle as the intensity increased. Air-support missions were flown. Add bone-chilling winds and you have a slight idea of what we had to endure to remain alive.

Another Day to Die

On Christmas Eve, 1944, in the vicinity of the Colmar Pocket, my squad ran up against a pack of radical German SS troops. The engagement quickly took on a savagery beyond belief. In time the Germans were forced into a battle-scarred building. They would not surrender. I and a few other members of our squad tossed grenades into the building, setting it on fire. We waited anxiously for the SS soldiers to come out and be annihilated. As the flames leaped higher and higher, we realized that they would never come out alive. You could hear the terrible death screams as the flames engulfed them. The stench of burning flesh was sickening. You hated to breathe for fear of throwing up.

We waited all night; and when morning arrived, the building gave a shudder and crashed to the ground. Nothing stirred; nothing moved. The 35 or so SS members would never be heard from again. Nothing was left but ashes.

We Don't Die Easily

Few of us thought about the true meaning of Christmas during these bloody, violent days. The concept "Peace on Earth" did not relate to those in the front lines. We only wanted to stay alive and kill, kill, kill more Germans.

The 3rd Infantry Division officially announced that

"the roast turkey, creamed potatoes, and other supplementary items which the Division Quartermaster had received for the Yule dinner was not to be consumed on Christmas Day by the 15th Regiment. On the contrary, the day was to be only another fierce episode which saw the Germans resisting with fanaticism."

I ate the usual C rations but the worst was that we did not have a drop of water for nearly two days. What a thirsty bunch of soldiers we were! I did have 2 turkey sandwiches several days later; so I did not miss my turkey completely. I only hope and pray that this is my last combat Christmas, but I had hoped for that in 1943 too. I honestly think the war will be over in 1945, (but does Hitler?)

Love to all,
Bob

There is one thing I can assure you happened on Christmas Day. The good Lord received thousands and thousands of prayers for peace on His birthday from this sector. It didn't make any difference what your faith was; no one cared. We were all together in this life and death struggle; your prayers were my prayers. And if per chance you felt the sting of death, we all died a little with you.

The "happy holiday" season continued.

It was in the Colmar sector that K Company lost an extraordinary number of brave men. There was a small, barren hill known as Hill 216 which overlooked a town. We were given orders to move up and take Hill #216. Easier said than done. Twice before Allied attempts to conquer #216 had ended in failure. The Germans were heavily dug in, full of determination, and of considerable strength. On top of the hill was a huge cross that looked over the land. That cross was our destination. My squad and I pushed our way upward ever so slowly with bullets singing all around. Our casualties quickly mounted. By some miracle, I made it near the crest. My lieutenant was a few yards in front of me. As I approached the lieutenant, I heard a murderous bark of a Jerry machine-gun. Looking up, I saw the knees of the lieutenant start to buckle. He went to his knees under the cross. A few seconds later there was another short burst from the German machine gun, and he toppled over into the dust. I kept firing and firing at anything that moved. Bullets ricocheted off my helmet. A staff sergeant with me tried to reach the lieutenant with this Tommy gun also blazing away, but he too fell beside his lieutenant under the cross. It was over! I could not make it alone. How I managed to work my way down the hill, I'll never know. My guardian angel certainly assisted me all the way. Our company was unable to conquer Hill #216. [It remained in German hands until the assault on Jan. 22, 1945 by the 254th Infantry.] We who fought so hard for Hill #216 will never forget those bloody days. When Christmas 1945 draws nigh, many of us will think back and wonder how we ever survived the Hill of Death. It was a miracle blessed in heaven.

> With Love to All and to All A Good Night,
> Bob

Dear Folks,

I would like to pass along a few thoughts my squad and I kicked around last evening during a lull in the fighting.

Several of my buddies were killed last week, and we were having a tough time keeping our spirits up. However, after our "pow-wow" we all felt better.

In general, we are so far away from home that we do not feel our family and friends have a true picture of the viciousness of war nor how extremely difficult it is to stay alive. All agree with me that we have been in actual combat too long without any relief; it is impossible to look forward to tomorrow. Most concurred that part of the problem lies with us. We do not want to worry our parents, wives, relatives, friends; so we continuously make light of our situation. The same holds true in combat when we strive not to show fear. It is time for families to reflect on the great sacrifices made by their loved ones in the cause of freedom. No one can ever comprehend the true meaning of sacrifice unless he or she is the individual making the sacrifice for others. We have chosen our destiny; the choice is ours alone. Do not despair for us. We will be together soon.

All my love,
Bob

January 18, 1945

Dear Folks,

Toward the end of December, 1944, I received a Christmas package that was a real lifesaver. My socks were just about ready for the junk heap (and I wasn't far behind). My feet were always freezing until one day I received Mary's box with socks in them. Did they come in handy! They were wonderful. I don't know how I could have survived without them; so please be sure and tell her they arrived at the most opportune time. I'll wear them until they cry for help; they are so easy on my feet. Unfortunately, my army-issued socks wear out in about two weeks. After that you are stuck with them unless you have another set (or lose a foot).

I have a pocket watch that works. The former owner, a German soldier, didn't have any use for it so he "donated" it to my cause. My old wristwatch is as sick as ever. As soon as I locate a new watchband, I'll strap it to my wrist as an ornament. That's all it was ever good for as far as I am concerned.

Ring Out the Old, Bring in the New

As the new year began, winter weather struck with all its fury. (No wonder Santa could not locate me.) Frostbite and trench foot casualties continued to mount. White for snow camouflage became the color of the day. Trying to stay alive was hard enough; but when you throw icy rivers to cross, nightly raiding patrols, rain, snow, and sub-zero temperatures at us, combined with strongly entrenched Germans and those dreaded artillery barrages and tanks, one can readily see the mix was far from "homey." It was pure HELL!

Chow Time!

"Baby, It's Cold Outside"

I have never tasted a winter like the one in the Vosges Mountains. The winter winds and blizzards of January were brutal. I had lived all my life in Rye, NY. The extreme cold in the Vosges was hard enough for me to endure, but our company's southern contingent really came close to freezing to death. Let's face it; no one could get warm in these surroundings, not even after the "heat of battles."

January 1945

Dear Folks,

I see you finally received the letter I wrote you in the middle of January 1945. I'll never forget those days in the Vosges Mountains! Many a night, I slept in covered foxholes and stood guard in blinding blizzards. Our company was so high in the mountains that we had to be supplied by pack mules. At night we put 3 blankets over our bodies and 2 under us to keep warm; it didn't solve the problem. We had an outpost on a hilltop that was fully manned every night. Guard duty was pulled outside the bunker where you were exposed to the bone-chilling winds; visibility was zero. On an hourly basis the soldier on guard was required to check-in with company headquarters some 100 yards to the rear. Those not on duty could try to catch some sleep inside the bunker which was completely enclosed except for an opening on one side. Blankets acted as a door to partially keep out "Jack Frost" and to prevent what little heat and light we had from escaping our castle.

The night I was in charge we had an extremely close call. A blizzard was raging; to stand duty outside in sub-zero temperatures was inhuman. I concluded no Germans could scale the mountain in such a violent snowstorm, and so I made the decision to pull guard duty inside the bunker; calls to headquarters would be hourly as ordered.

Sometime after midnight the guard on duty woke me and gave me the bad news—our communications wire had been cut. The Krauts had crept up the mountain and were in the vicinity. To liquidate us the Germans had merely to toss a grenade or two into our bunker. Our squad would have been wiped out in seconds. A real bad decision on my part wouldn't you say?

I quickly slipped out of the bunker, fully expecting to be met by a volley of gunfire. Nothing!! Unbelievable!! It was snowing so hard I could not see more than a few feet. I knew the Germans were laying probably in the snow somewhere nearby as I was checking the wire to locate the trouble, but it was impossible to see them or vis-à-vis. It was time for my squad to vacate the outpost and pull back to the company's main line-of-resistance.

The following night our captain decided the outpost was far too dangerous and did not carry much in the way of military value; no one was sent to man the outpost. That was a lucky break because the Jerries returned that night in force. The bunker was empty. However, next morning we found tracks all over the place. That day we hid mines and booby traps as a surprise for the Germans if they returned.

Love to All,
Bob

Dear Gang,

I want to explain some of my experiences to you. The action in combat takes place so fast and unexpectedly that it's often over before you know it; before you think much of it. After you realize what transpired, you wonder how you ever escaped injury or death. Also every moment of combat is dangerous; so you must expect many narrow escapes. It became an ongoing feeling/sensation to have a close shave at least twice a week when we were on the attack. However, in the Vosges

Mountains and Colmar Pocket it was ten times as dangerous as any other place. It seemed every minute or two in these sectors you would be hitting the ground to escape feeling the hot pang of a bullet or shrapnel. You had to be on guard every second.

All My Love,
Bob

When I enlisted in the army, I cannot recall anything in my job description that remotely resembled my true life as a combat infantryman. Wait! There was one thing that never changed. I was covered by insurance in case of death up to the maximum amount of $10,000. (Premiums paid by yours truly.)

This job left much to be desired, starting with the pay scale. The extra $10 for combat pay was definitely not worth it. Hopefully, the new year would bring a few extra greenbacks my way. I should have made sergeant (without the "acting"). I had earned it many times over.

There Is No Rest for the Weary

There is an old saying, which applies directly to the 3rd Infantry Division. It goes something like this: "when you have a good thing going, don't change horses in mid-stream." Our division (the horse) was riding high on victories; we were unbeatable! Notwithstanding the fact that fatigue was beginning to overtake us, our commanders in mid-January decided to pull the division back from the front lines, give our nerves a shot of adrenalin, and prepare us for the final major offensive in France: the elimination of the Colmar Pocket. Training was to be brief. Commencement date was set for January 22, 1945. (Does the time period sound familiar? It should. It was the anniversary date of our invasion of Anzio in 1944.)

Let the Battle Begin:
The Dramatic Conclusion of the Colmar Pocket

Our regiment's attack caught the Germans completely by surprise, as did the 254th Infantry's assault on Hill 216. For once and for all Hill 216 was in the hands of the Allies. Within days our company had crossed the L'Ill River, smashed our way through various French towns, and cleared out a few scattered enemy forces north of the Colmar Canal. On the evening of January 29th, our entire regiment waited on the banks of the Canal in rubber boats. Unlike Anzio, we did not spin our wheels aimlessly. We crossed the canal, and once again the drive to the Rhine River and Germany was underway.

Dig We Must

Dear Folks,

A couple of days ago I told you about my pal, Travis Mann from Texas, returning to the States. In France, we used to "bunk" together in a foxhole when we were in combat. I was lost without him in the Colmar assault. He was relieved of combat duty and sent to the mail room during the drive.

I was an awful lazy cuss when it came to digging foxholes for protection. I'd rather sleep out in the open than dig a hole to crawl in. Travis was entirely different. He'd always scratch out a foxhole for both of us. Many a night artillery shells would land close by; I would be safe thanks to Travis. I even threw away my entrenching shovel at St. Die, France and didn't pick up another until the push into Germany. What a fool! Thanks to Travis' "ambition," I was saved more than once. He, though, was much more nervous than I; so he would always say he felt better when I was with him, cracking stories. This arrangement worked out for the best for both of us. I was delighted to see him leave when he did.

All my Love,
"Lonesome" Bob

The wiping out of the Colmar Pocket was exceedingly brutal, to put it mildly. We had continual night assaults, and the snow only helped slow us down. On many occasions we had to cross wide open areas with no cover from deadly German machine gun and artillery fire. All that you could do was keep low and pray you would get by unscratched.

I always felt our battle plans were similar in many respects to a game of chess. Our next play belonged to all units of the 3rd Infantry Division and culminated in the fall of Neuf-Brisach and the capture (intact) of the vital bridge sites spanning the Rhine River. As we approached the city, the fighting became extremely ferocious. It appeared as though Neuf-Brisach was going to be quite difficult to subdue. Suddenly, the moves (battle plans) were changed. A miracle was played out, and the city capitulated without a fight. The official 3rd Infantry Division records describe the battle as follows:

> [The entire fort] fell with hardly a fight to two patrols. One patrol group was led by a civilian through a 60-foot tunnel under the town's protecting wall and moat and up in the center of town. The other patrol dropped into the dry moat and crossed into town while the enemy slept. The surprised Germans gave up without a scrap.

How sweet is the taste of victory.

With the capture of Neuf-Brisach on February 7, 1945, the accolades began to flow freely. After 188 days of non-stop combat, the 3rd Infantry Division was relieved of frontline duty. Rotating rest camps were established.

Presidential Unit Citation

The 3rd Infantry Division became the first American division to receive the coveted Presidential Citation for their distinguished accomplishments "during the period 22nd January to 6th February 1945."

I sent my family a copy of our division citation that appeared in our newspaper. It stated,

> Fighting through heavy snow storms, across flat land raked by 88mm, 120mm mortar, artillery, tank and machine-gun fire, through enemy-infested marshes and woods, the 3rd Division breached the German defense wall on the northern perimeter of the Colmar Bridgehead and drove forward to isolate Colmar from the Rhine.
>
> Crossing the Fecht River from Guemar, Alsace, by stealth at 2100 hours on 22nd January 1945, assault elements of the 3rd Division fought their way forward against mounting enemy resistance. When the bridge constructed across the L'Ill River collapsed before supporting armor could arrive on the far side, two heroic battalions of the 30th Infantry Regiment held tenaciously to their small foothold across the stream against furious, tank-supported enemy attacks.

Let me pause a moment to reflect on the gravity of the L'Ill River situation. Here it was in the dead of winter, snowing, with temperatures ranging in the minus figures.

The 30th Regiment had been badly mauled and needed time to reorganize; K company and another company from the 15th Regiment were rushed into the struggle after the 2nd battalion of the 30th was beaten back. I and members of my squad, fully clothed, crossed the icy river and joined the isolated and outnumbered troops of the 30th Regiment. Previously, I related to you how some Jerry tanks overran our positions, and we were forced back into the river to save our lives.

While discussing this citation, the *History of the Third Infantry Division* stressed that a "good proportion of the entire regiment was nearly frozen from its terrible exposure to the Ill River and the icy blasts of wind which greeted the men as they clambered from the water."

Headquarters was determined to retake the bridgehead. The Germans were equally determined to hold their positions. The situation was extremely bleak. Everyone was soaking wet and frozen; there was no place to dry off. Dry clothes were desperately needed along with supporting armor.

That same night the order was given to "move out." Once again we forded the icy river; despite being totally outnumbered, we were able to secure and hold the bridgehead.

Official records indicate that during this period the 3rd Infantry Division "destroyed three entire German divisions and badly mauled another. A total of 21,353 officers and enlisted men were entitled to wear the blue Presidential unit badge."

CHAPTER 9

A Time to Rest and Reflect

February 8, 1945

Dear Folks,

Golly, it's great to be at the rest camp for four days. Now, I can catch up on my sleep and all the letters I owe everyone. While at the camp I decided to have a tooth fixed that for ages had been aching me. The problem was quickly solved. When I left the dentist's chair, I was once again minus a tooth. I had plenty of other bad ones, but couldn't have them all fixed at this time. (One to a customer.) I certainly hope I don't lose too many more before the war is over.

So Gene finally came overseas. I thought he'd make it. His infantry division, the 36th, was shipped over some time ago and have already fought beside us. Perhaps I'll have a chance to see him when this fighting is finally over. "Red" is also fairly close by, but I can't figure out just where he is located.

I have a $40 money order that I'm sending you. I sold a German pistol a while ago. As soon as we went on the attack in January, I "found" another one.

A Gourmet Delight

Dear Twenty-Three,

In one of daddy's booklets on life in Rye, he inquired about what our daily meal menu looks like in the infantry. Basically, anyone except a combat man gets pretty decent meals, but while we are in combat, [which was almost always] we have to be content with C or K rations. For a long time the only C rations the government had available were stew, hash, and beans. The biscuits were nothing to rave about either because they were hard (like hockey pucks). At last someone woke up to the fact that few ate all their rations; so today we are given the new C rations. The menu includes meat and noodles, franks and beans, ham and eggs, stew, meat and beans, and spaghetti. Of that selection, we go for the "franks" best and then the "noodles, and meat and beans." Quite a lot lean toward the spaghetti, but not too many. Stew is the one can that almost no one ever touches. It's always been on our blacklist and always will be. The best improvement has been with the biscuit unit. You can at least digest and enjoy them (to a degree) without throwing up.

There are 3 meals daily—breakfast, dinner and supper. Besides the above menu breakfast includes coffee, a small portion of a compressed cereal, a small bag of peanuts, and 4 biscuits. The cereal is the best addition; so naturally the breakfast unit is the most popular. The dinner includes lemon and has 5 biscuits and sometimes a small container of jam. Unfortunately, the jam isn't in every unit; only a few have jam.

I eat breakfast and dinner and a can of franks and beans if I can get one. You see, the Army ships enough food for 8 soldiers in each ration container. However, for some inexplicable reason, there are only 4 cans of franks and beans in a container. Does that make any sense?

Along with each day's rations, you receive a pack of cigarettes and a tiny chocolate bar. As a rule bread is sent up; but if we're on the move, we cannot be bothered taking it along.

The best part of our whole nightly ration distribution is the mail bag. That's what we really go for no matter how dog-tired we are. Mail and care packages from home certainly do build up your morale, and I am not kiddin'. Keep 'em coming!

With Love to All,
Bob

In February 1945, the Commanding General of the 1st French Army publicly recognized the 3rd Infantry Division's outstanding role in the Vosges/Colmar areas and "awarded the division its second Croix de Guerre citation, entitling the men to wear the coveted fourragere."

February 18, 1945

Dear Folks,

I have finally found out what happened to my bonds and why we weren't getting them each month. It seems the army changed the pay system without notifying anyone. Henceforth, you will not receive any bonds until I actually get paid. Many times I don't receive my pay for 2–3 months due to combat conditions. You won't get any bonds in these instances. (This doesn't seem proper since I've earned my pay.)

I've had several letters from Mrs. Law and Russell. She's awfully nice to me, always telling me to include a request for cookies so she can send them. I don't ever request anything, but I try to write them both whenever I get a chance. She told me how Russell had his heart set on seeing you. Unfortunately, along came the mix up concerning school; so he had to remain in Illinois.

Had several cute valentine cards from Ann, Alyce Sloat, and the gang. To tell the truth, I hadn't even remembered Valentine's Day until the cards came rolling by.

Incidentally, don't send anymore bedeviled ham. I don't care for it too much. We in the army always have a great joke over anything that looks like spam. The army generally feeds you so much of that stuff that you get to hate the sight of it. When we get pork luncheon meat to eat, we turn up our nose and pass.

I'm glad your mail packages are coming over so much faster. Thanks loads for writing and care packages. They are great to receive.

Love to All,
Bob

"Sorry, I'm Too Busy"

February 23, 1945

Dear Folks,

I don't know whether or not you agree with me, but a piece of news that I read today seems to be hushed up. I'm wondering how the papers in the States treated the note of apology that General de Gaulle sent President Roosevelt for not being able to meet him. The *Stars and Stripes* [published in France] hardly mentioned it. I suppose if the facts were played up, it would create hard feelings. I don't pretend to know much about politics, but if the leading statesman of a country ever wrote me (the President) a note saying he was "too busy" at the moment to attend a conference (but they were not too busy to accept our help), then I'd really clamp down on them.

You were right about where our division was fighting. I notice the papers in the States keep you up-to-date on the whereabouts of the various outfits. It's funny but we are never allowed to mention our location. However, the papers in the States can print any news which comes their way. It's a crazy world, isn't it? Freedom of the press, I presume. Will write you in a day or two.

Love to All,
Bob

Reminiscing

As the new year rolled along, the strains of battle were beginning to have a decided impact on me. It was becoming extremely difficult to keep my spirits up day in and day out in the Vosges Mountains. My days in actual combat would soon exceed 330 without any relief in sight. I had had entirely too many days in combat and I was becoming discouraged; would the killing never end? What future did I have as a combat infantryman? Death probably.

I wrote my parents on February 20, 1945:

It burns me up to have so many men in the armed forces having plush jobs all the time while we in the infantry are expected to do all the fighting all the time. The top brass never think of giving a combat soldier a break. You just press forward until you fall, and it will happen. You have absolutely nothing in the world to look forward to except keep fighting your heart out until this war is over. The only rest you get is when you are wounded and end up in the hospital. Yes, the infantryman carries a heavy burden with no personal goal or objective to strive to achieve. (Other than victory on the battlefield.) The Air Corps allocates so many flying missions after which the pilot gets a reward, but do they do that in the infantry? No! And that's what burns us up!

"Angry,"
Bob

March 2, 1945

Dear Folks,

Mrs. Law certainly is up-to-date in regard to our troop movements. She hits the nail on the head every time as to where we have been fighting.

I took a chance and sent my watch to Paris to be fixed. The Red Cross in Paris does the work. If it is at all possible, the watch might return to active duty. I only hope it is returned to me. If it doesn't start ticking this time, the watch will receive a dishonorable discharge and be shipped back to you.

Love to All,
Bob

Dear Folks,

I just started to read Ernie Pyle's story. It starts with the invasion of Sicily when Ernie tags along as a war correspondent. As I read some of the passages, I could not help but remember how I felt going into combat. When I knew I was about to enter into combat for the first time, I made up my mind that I would never either say or show I was afraid. And so it was, my comrades used to think I had iron nerves even though I was just as nervous at times as anyone. When shells would be landing close by and fellows hitting the ground, I would just keep going and giving encouragement as if nothing had happened. That was until I reached the Vosges Mountains and got hit. After being wounded, I had more sense and grew more cautious. The only thing I never changed was digging a foxhole. Generally, I would not scratch out a foxhole no matter what the circumstances. I just did not have the ambition, and usually I was too tired to bother. Sgt. Travis Mann used to rescue me in this situation. We'd always "bunk" together, using both blankets and our body heat to keep warm.

Russell was just like me in regard to showing emotions and that is why we bonded together so well. He always liked to horse around as I did; so we had many good times together. (If any time in combat could be listed as "good.") Russell joined K company the same day I did and was in the same tent that I hung out. We both hated to pull guard duty at night; so we volunteered for night patrols. If we went out on patrol, we would not have to pull guard duty when (and if) we returned safely. Gradually, with so many close calls on patrol, we had some sense knocked into our heads, and we quit volunteering. I hardly went on patrol after Russell was wounded.

Of all the tough places I've been in combat, I'd say the Vosges Mountains were the worst. We had more men go completely out of their minds ("battle fatigue") there than any other campaign. It was not unusual in a company to have 5 or 6 soldiers a day go nuts, and that includes officers as well as enlisted men. It is simply terrible to see grown men laying in the dirt, crying, and screaming their lungs out. They could stand no more terror, and their minds cracked under the strain. Most would recover in due time, but the majority never returned to the infantry. I recall various instances whereby a lot of real tough soldiers just threw down their arms and could go on no more. Some of my close friends broke down and had to be taken away. Although my nerves were often worn raw, I just could not quit. A hundred times I said to myself that I could take no more; but when the attack and the adrenalin began to flow, I seemed to change and was ready to press forward. I would continuously say to myself that as soon as I was relieved, I would request reclassification. Of course, I never did. I was in the infantry "till death do us part." I never let the thought of being killed bother me.

Say, haven't I been talking a long time about the war and how I felt. There is no one alive who can say he wasn't afraid during actual combat. Some can suppress their feelings while others just come out and shake all over. In K company, we had a great sergeant. He never exhibited any feelings on how he felt until he came to the Vosges. One day he simply told the captain he could not continue. Eventually, he was reclassified. It happens every day in combat, although many are just plain scared and will not join in the attack. These soldiers don't seem to realize that the man next to him is not any happier about the situation but has enough will power to move on. Quite a few soldiers will disappear during a firefight and turn up after all is over. They are the ones that burn us up because in 9 out of 10 cases, they will go to the hospital and be reclassified. The rest of us keep plugging along and hoping for the best; we are the real heroes of the war. It is to these men that Ernie Pyle wrote and dedicated his book.

Hum-m-m! This decidedly is enough on the war. Once I begin I don't know when to stop. I don't know how interesting it is to you, but it will give you an idea of what goes on in the mind of a combat soldier. A boy stationed in the Pacific is no different than those in Europe.

I like your idea of putting the comics in my care boxes. *Blondie, Captain and the Kids,* and *Prince Valiant* are always some of my favorites. Please keep sending them with your cookies.

With Love to All,
"The Cookie King"

March 11, 1945

Dear Folks,

The mailman hit me heavy today. Now, I'll have to get busy and answer the entire crew of budding authors.

Russell wrote me about college. His classes are not very large, and they are "dominated" by women. He likes it a lot. Can't blame him. He's in heaven, finally.

I read where Patton addressed some grammar school children and told them they would be the "warriors of the future." Patton thinks there will be another war too. No matter how hard we try to maintain peace, I am afraid that someday the armies will start marching again, and we'll have to go through more misery than anyone ever dreamed possible.

Love to All,
Bob

CHAPTER 10

Germany

3rd Infantry Division Timetable in Germany and Austria

Date	Description
1945	
Mar 14	3rd Infantry Division reaches border of Germany.
Mar 15	Division crosses border into Germany.
Mar 19	Siegfried Line pierced. I was relieved of frontline combat duty and transferred to regiment's military police (MP) unit.
Mar 26–Mar 27	Rhine River crossed near Worms.
Mar 30	7th Army (including 3rd Infantry Division) reassigned to 6th Army Group and ordered to southeast Germany.
Apr 17–Apr 25	Nurnberg officially surrenders; 3rd Infantry Division prepares to strike Munich.
Apr 26–Apr 27	Small town of Unter Thurheim captured, thereby freeing 52 Americans (some of the 3rd Infantry Division) who had been captured in Anzio.
Apr 30	Munich falls. Closing days of war follow.
May 2–May 3	Salzburg entered; Berchtesgaden falls.
May 5	End of hostilities.
May 7	European phase of WWII ends at Reims, France.
Jun 6	3rd Infantry Division becomes first American infantry division to receive the Presidential Unit Citation for outstanding performance in combat during the period of January 22–February 6, 1945 (eliminating the Colmar Pocket).

The Final Bridge Is Crossed

On March 13, 1945, the 3rd Infantry Division was poised to start their assault on German soil. There was no doubt in our minds; this was the beginning of the end of the brutal Hitler regime. Orders were relayed to us from headquarters; the attack on Germany would commence on March 15, 1945. No passports were required. Nothing could stop us!

Smashing the Siegfried Line

K company began their opening drive from an area near Saarbrucken. Bitter fighting ensued. However, we were on a roll; the "die is cast." Before you could blink your eyes, a section of the once so-called "indestructible/impregnable" Siegfried fortification was breached. Our next immediate targets were Kaiserslautern and the Rhine River. It took us only 2 1/2 days from the time we left Kaiserslautern to cross the Rhine and begin our mad dash through Germany. Large numbers of surrendering, young German soldiers began to pour in; deserters and stragglers, likewise, decided enough is enough.

During this period, our planes continuously flew over German positions and saturated the area with "surrender" instructions. Many captured Germans carried these papers in their pockets or waved them at us so we would not shoot them.

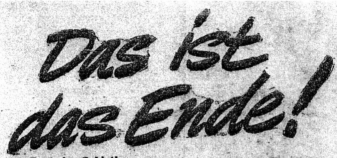

Das ist das Ende!

Deutscher Soldat!

Du hast jetzt gesehen, was die Ueberlegenheit der Alliierten an Menschen und Material bedeutet. Du wirst das Schicksal Deiner Kameraden von Stalingrad, Tunis und Cherbourg teilen. Du wirst eingekesselt, zusammengeschossen und vernichtet werden.

Die Wuerfel sind gefallen. Der Sieg der Alliierten ist sicher. Willst Du sterben, ohne der deutschen Sache nutzen zu koennen? Ist es nicht besser, sich zu ergeben und gesund zu den Deinen zurueckzukehren?

Nachstehender Passierschein gibt Dir die Moeglichkeit, Dich ohne Gefahr ergeben zu koennen. Du wirst behandelt werden, wie es einem Soldaten gebuehrt. Du wirst nach Hause zurueckkommen und teilnehmen am Wiederaufbau Deutschlands.

| Safe-conduct | **PASSIERSCHEIN** | Laissez-passer |

Der deutsche Soldat, der diesen Passierschein vorzeigt, hat den ehrlichen Willen, sich zu ergeben. Er ist zu entwaffnen. Er hat Anspruch auf anstaendige Behandlung und Verpflegung und, wenn noetig, aerztliche Hilfe. Er muss so rasch wie moeglich aus der Gefahrenzone entfernt werden.

Oberkommandierender der Alliierten Armeen im Mittelmeerraum

To Allied troops.
The German soldier displaying this pass shows his honest intention of surrendering. He is to be disarmed, treated fairly, fed, given medical attention if necessary, and removed as soon as possible from the danger-zone.

H. M. WILSON
Supreme Allied Commander,
Mediterranean Theatre.

Aux troupes alliées.
Le soldat allemand porteur de ce laissez-passer montre son intention honnête de se rendre. Il doit être désarmé, traité comme il convient, nourri, soigné par un médecin en cas de besoin, et éloigné de la zone de danger dans le plus bref délai.

H. M. WILSON
Commandant suprême allié,
Zone de la Méditerranée.

AF/148

Surrender Leaflets Dropped on Germans

A Gift of Life: March 19, 1945

One of the most important days of my life and one I will never forget was March 19, 1945. I was exhausted after being involved throughout the entire day in an intense firefight with the Germans. My nerves were shattered. The battle spread over into the night. Prisoners continued to drift in. Without any advance notice, I was pulled aside that evening and instructed to report to company headquarters immediately. Now what had I done? My squad was in excellent condition, we all meshed beautifully, and to my knowledge I had not recently stepped too far out of line. However, you never know what to expect in wartime. Probably some comment I made. It was, therefore, with great trepidation that I reported to headquarters, fully expecting the worse.

At first I couldn't believe what I was hearing. It was a shock heard around the world. No one was more astonished than I upon being informed that I was being relieved of my duties as "acting squad leader" and transferred to regimental military police (MP) unit. I couldn't believe my good fortune. My prayers had been answered; my combat days were over. No more killing. I had miraculously survived Mt. Cassino, Anzio, Southern France, the Vosges Mountains, and the Colmar Pocket, as well as two first-wave amphibious landings, being left behind enemy lines, and being wounded. My squad, platoon, and friends could not believe the good news either. Another Lynch joke, many thought. Here I was, 22 years old with more combat experience than probably anyone in my company, and I was finally saying goodbye and walking away with my life intact. My guardian angel and I could sit back and feel the stress leave our bodies (both human and heavenly). Oh yes, mine is the human one, if I may boast a bit.

V-mail dated March 19, 1945

My new mailing address is Regimental Hdq. Co. 15th Inf. APO3, c/o PM. N.Y., N.Y. It's really a great break for me.

News from Home

March 1945

I had a letter from Rosemary this past week. She wrote a nice long letter telling me all the "exciting" happenings in Rye. Ann wrote and told me Charlie Mitchell was killed. After 2 months without a word, I heard from Doug Ward. He was in Belgium when the Germans broke through our lines. Apparently, Doug was severely wounded but is on the road to recovery. He wrote and told me he has seen enough fighting to last a lifetime too.

I also received a news bulletin from Jean Wahl. It was a short paper all about our class members. It seems that Lou Angelilli is still back in the States. (The lucky fellow.) Most of my classmates are starting to trickle abroad. By the time the ones coming to the European theater arrive in France, it will be curtain time. (The war will be over.)

I realize you are pretty busy these days with Christmas only 264 days away.

Luff 'n' stuff,
Bob

March 23, 1945

Dear Folks,

My mail from the States has started to arrive regularly again. I had a stack of letters from everyone dropped at my abode. I notice you sent the baked beans I longed for. That's swell. I know I'll like them. However, I won't need anything like that in the future. I now receive hot food instead of C rations; so I won't be starving as I was in combat. My stomach hasn't heard of the transfer to the MPs and is finding the warm meals a little hard to digest. I sent my new address to the Rye contingent.

Mrs. Law and Russell continue to keep my spirits up with weekly letters on life in the good 'ole U.S.A. I'm anxious to find out how Russell adapts to college life after all he's been through. Perhaps someday I'll have to roll up my sleeves and return to the books and get my degree. I wonder how many credits NYU will bestow on me for my extracurricular work in Europe? I understand Gene White wants to enroll for a year in college when he comes home.

'Bye for a while,
Bob

Battle Rankings: The Most Vicious Campaigns

I had always felt the Anzio campaign was the most savage and most terrifying battlefield I ever encountered. However, after crossing the Vosges Mountains and smashing the Colmar Pocket, I changed my ratings. I wrote the following letter on July 20, 1945:

The President's citation as well as the French Croix de Guerre with palm is for our work in the Colmar Pocket. As far as the terror and fighting goes, the Vosges Mountains were the worst; Colmar came in a clear second and Anzio third. I'd much rather have to go back to Anzio than to cross the Vosges Mountains again. From my letters you've read how exceedingly brutal Anzio was; so you can imagine what Vosges and Colmar were like. One of our highest-ranked officers got battle fatigue in the Vosges along with hundreds of other officers and men. When you get so many stress injuries like that, you know it's wicked!

Still Smiling, Still Shaking,
Bob

My guardian angel worked overtime for me that year (1945). He kept me alive and kicking so I could complete the Colmar drive. It was time for him to relax a mite, perhaps take a sabbatical leave. He had earned it. My final tabulation days in combat stood at 330–355. It is interesting to note that official sources have determined "the average soldier can endure no more than 240 days of combat before going mad." Where does that leave me?

A Typical Ravaged German Town

The Vanquished

March 29, 1945

Dear Folks,

As we push through German cities, one can't help noticing all the white flags that fly from each house. Just about everyone has a white sheet or towel hanging from an upstairs window. Long before we reach a town or city, the people get ready and unwrap their white sheets. When we arrive all the windows and doors are closed tight and the Nazis' insignias and flags are gone for good.

I'm sure I forgot to mention it, but I had another great box of candy from the Hershey Company via 23 Oakwood Avenue. Last month I had been munching on German chocolates that I "found." I think the captured Germans had just received their PX rations when I breezed upon the scene with guns blazing. Their chocolates weren't too bad, especially if you don't have any; but they don't compare with our own milk chocolate. The Kraut chocolate isn't as sweet as ours. As a matter of fact, I haven't tasted any real Jerry milk chocolate that's very good.

I had two letters from Ruthie recently. She was going to shoot me if I didn't send her a V-mail soon. I hadn't written her in over a month but that could not be helped; can't stop the war to write. I carry around a list of dates when I wrote such 'n' such a person; so I know exactly who I am behind in writing. I always try to write you, Gene, and Ann once a week, if possible, but you know how difficult it was most of the times. Someday when the war is over, things will be a little easier, and I will be able to write and visit everyone.

Dear Frenchie,

Lately I've had quite a few letters and V-mail from you. I like to read your manuscripts telling me about the news from the neighborhood. I see you still listen to *The Lone Ranger* and the same ole murder and mystery stories (*The Shadow Knows, Green Hornet*) on the radio that we used to hear together.

"Au revoir,"
Robert

"Onward and Upward"

After crossing the Rhine River our regiment was soon in the neighborhood of Schweinfort, home of the Germans great ball-bearing factory.

As the regiment drove onward, the highways became scattered with mangled bodies of animals and disabled or abandoned German equipment that had been caught by our artillery or air support. In general, German resistance was slight; small fire-fights were encountered by front-line troops in a few towns along the road to Hitler's once proud city of Nurnberg.

During the 3rd Infantry Division's advance, our air corps had commenced a saturation bombing of Nuremberg. By April 20th when the huge city capitulated, more than half the city was in ruins. From Nuremberg our regiment kept pressing southward, crossed the Danube and entered Augsburg (population 200,000) practically without a fight. The credit for the capture of the entire city on April 28th went to my old K Company. The city was hardly touched by the war. After a two-day stay to catch our breath (and a few German soldiers), we headed for the biggest prize of them all—Munich. All three Allied divisions arrived at approximately the same time in Munich. The 3rd Infantry Division flew through so fast we couldn't see much of the damage. However, we did realize the war was rapidly drawing to a close; it was a matter of days. There was no official surrender at Munich; the German officials had already left.

There remained two more important places for the 3rd to conquer. In early May the first major city to fall into the 3rd Infantry Division's hands was Salzburg (Austria), followed by Hitler's fortress—Berchtesgaden. If Hitler had expected to make a final stand at Berchtesgaden, he would not have had a chance. The air corps destroyed the city. Every building was either completely leveled to the ground or partially bombed out. The underground caves, though, could still be entered easily. In the caves were regular living quarters and modern equipment. There were great storerooms full of misappropriated valuable paintings, exquisite Chinaware, and other extremely valuable objects of art.

> While I was in Berchtesgaden, I took some pictures of the caves, artifacts etc. As soon as I get the negatives, I'll send them to you to be developed. So long for now. I'll tell you more in my next letter.
>
> With Love to All,
> Bob

April 15, 1945

Dear Pals,

I sent a few more souvenirs home this week. There were several German medals and a Luftwaffe (Air Force) jacket. I thought you would like to see what an actual German uniform looks like. I must admit the

Air Force jacket is the smartest looking one of them all. It is a real dressy German uniform.

The little skulls I sent Willie signified that the one who wore them was in the tank corps. The tank men sport an all-black uniform with skulls on the collar. The infantrymen always have a greenish-blue uniform.

You can tell the branch of service of a German soldier by the piping on his collar and shoulder. A thin, white, thread-like material sewn on his collar tells you he is in the infantry while a red one indicates artillery.

Shoulder straps indicate the soldier's grade. An all-white braid points out a lieutenant. If he has only white braid around the edges, you know he is a sergeant. By adding a pip to the braids, you increase his grade. You probably don't understand this brilliant presentation but it is important to us when capturing German troops.

April 21, 1945

Dear Folks,

I am sure you have read in the newspapers about the former prisoners of war that all armies are freeing. We have run across our share of them too. Of course, they are immensely happy. Most cannot believe they are actually free to return home after all these years in German captivity.

I have met plenty of Australian and Englishmen along the way. They call us "the bloody Yanks" and cannot give enough praise to our air corps, tanks, and infantrymen. As for the soldiers themselves, the Australians agree the Americans are tops in toughness and fighting ability. The man most discussed is Patton and his tank corps; Montgomery runs a close second.

Although the war is rapidly drawing to a close, whenever the German populace hear a plane, they rush to their basements or shelters even though the plane may be German. That's how much the Germans have grown to fear our air corps! They say they live in dread of being bombed and strafed.

Oh yes! Daddy wrote me about the biggest home-front scoop of the year. I understand he cut the grass. WOW!

With Love to All;
"Green with Envy,"
Bob

April 29, 1945

Dear Folks,

I seem to have received a lot of mail recently, including a couple of letters from Ann. In one letter she writes as a young girl and in the other as a mature woman. Roosevelt had passed away, and it was a great blow to her as it was to the world. When we heard the news, we couldn't believe it possible that the President had died. Truman certainly has a huge burden to shoulder.

Several days later, we read in the newspaper that Ernie Pyle [foreign correspondent] had lost his life too. I think Ernie was one man who was universally liked and admired by everyone in the Armed Forces. It's too bad both could not have been around when hostilities finally grind to a close. I'll be there but many of my friends will not.

Love to All,
Bob

May 2, 1945
Dear Civilians,

Another letter from you, and I see we have the usual mix-up in the mail. If the mail didn't get muddled up, it wouldn't be natural. I wouldn't know what to do. I may as well tell you once again about my M.P. job in case my original letters never reach Rye.

In the M.P.s, we do a lot of guarding captured German soldiers, directing regimental traffic, and watching our own equipment to see it doesn't walk away. One night we were sent to locate a sniper whom we did not find. One of the greatest benefits of the job is that we eat hot chow whenever possible. Consequently I've gained a little weight (one pound two ounces). As a combat infantryman, my weight ranged between 120-140 pounds. Now it is 140 of pure muscle.

While I write, peace rumors are flying thick and fast. By the time this letter reaches the States, the war in Europe will be over. The German soldiers are surrendering by hundreds. They keep telling us it is useless to keep fighting. Some of these soldiers are old, old men with one eye gone or have a wooden leg. Others are so young; they haven't learned to use a razor. Their ages run from 12 to 50, but as far as we are concerned, they are German soldiers and can shoot a gun if given a chance. I have no compassion for any of them. The SS troops are the worst. They are the real arrogant Nazi type and deserve no mercy. You have undoubtedly read about the concentration camps maintained by the SS. They are real!!

All my Love,
Bob

"9 to 5"

May 6, 1945
Dear Pals at "23,"

I'm afraid Daddy doesn't understand how combat soldiers operate. He wonders whether or not my hours in the MPs are shorter than as a combat man. When you are in combat, you basically are always in the line-of-fire and on the alert 24 hours a day; you must be ready to move into the attack at any minute, day or night. If you are not on the offensive at the moment, guard duty beckons to prevent Germans from moving in fast and counter-attacking. Patrol duty is always calling; sleep is placed on the back burner. In general, you are not able to even catch a "catnap." However, if you are exceedingly lucky and manage to ensnare a little shuteye in your foxhole, you will find yourself being roused at 2 or 3 in the morning and instructed to pack and get ready to move on to the next objective. During these times, you are so sleepy you can hardly find your own equipment. Eventually, you gather your thoughts together and await the attack order. You eat on the run; there are no bathroom facilities. You have no life to call your own.

Life in the MPs is entirely different. We still have guard duty; but when we are off-duty, we can seize some sleep in a bed/cot or do whatever we please. It's extremely difficult to snooze in the daytime; so in reality, we never get enough sleep. These past weeks the division has been moving so rapidly across Germany that, usually, we would be on the move in trucks all day. At night we would stop, eat a hot meal, pull guard duty, and be off again early in the morning. That is why my letter writing has dropped to a trickle. Once the fighting has officially ceased, I will be a little better off and will write more often.

Ah yes! I read your French letter; without any problem. Now I'm on a German kick. Auf Wiedersehen. The end is near.

Your sleepy Head,
Bob

May 7, 1945

Dear Folks,

Looking back, I think I am about the worst man who ever walked this earth when it comes to sewing. I couldn't sew a patch on my uniform correctly, so my pal Travis Mann had to help me most of the time. He was pretty "sharp" with a needle; so I'd call on him to bail me out. We both were squad leaders in K Company. The only difference was he was promoted to Sergeant, and I had to be content as "acting squad leader." Same job, same authority, same number of soldiers under one's control. Leadership qualities varied somewhat; I was more easygoing; Travis was a soldier's soldier.

Love to All,
PFC Bob

CHAPTER 11

The War in Europe Is Over

At 2:41 a.m. on Monday, May 7, 1945 at Reims, France, the European phase of World War II officially came to a conclusion.

Austria: "C'est Finis!"

May 13, 1945

Dear Gang,

The war has been over for 6 days. The guns are silent; civilians are rejoicing in the streets. It is a great feeling to know the hostilities have ceased, but individual feelings still run strong.

The sun is shining in all its glory on this Mother's Day. I would say it is finally getting warm. Last year I was at Anzio, and this year I walked and rode my way through France, Germany, and Austria. I don't think I told you the 3rd had entered Austria. All the people seem to have taken their Austrian flags out of mothballs and exhibit them proudly. Many times these people or soldiers ask me whether we distinguish them from the Germans. We are not Germans, they emphasize; We are Austrians! It's always the same story. They didn't want to fight us; they were forced into the war. Today they want to be our friends. Their logic runs as follows: They fought us, but it was SS troops who drove them into combat. They keep telling us if they did not fight alongside the Germans, their families would be tortured.

When you see the SS sign around, you know that the SS troops had been in the area. These soldiers wear their insignia on their helmets, uniforms, vehicles, and probably their underwear and socks. They really thought they were supermen from the word go.

There is a story a German officer related to me that I thought you might find amusing. Of course, he exaggerates a bit, but the fundamental principle is there. He told me how the Germans spent weeks constructing road blocks to halt our advance, but they were useless. "It took the Americans 40 minutes to destroy them. For 39 minutes they [Americans] would stand, scrutinize the roadblock, and laugh; the next minute they would crush the obstruction."

When we knew the war in Europe was officially over, we were all extremely relieved. We could see it coming and expected it any day.

Finally, we were advised the armistice was signed, and the Krauts had surrendered. However, we were notified the news wouldn't be distributed to the press until a certain date. I can imagine how the radios must have interrupted all U.S. programs to give you the news flash. It doesn't seem much different to me now. Europe is full of bombed cities and white crosses. You can walk through the endless rows of crosses and wonder to yourself what it would be like if there was to be another war. More crosses!!

With All my Love,
Bob

Point System

May 17, 1945

Dear Folks,

Since the war is over, we've been discussing our point-discharge system. Until the official announcement was released, we were wondering how much credit we would receive for combat days. When the final calculations were published, we were crushed! We found that once again the infantrymen had been forgotten. We do not get a single extra point for combat! All the sacrifices and hardships we endured day in and day out meant hardly nothing. It's true, battle stars count a lot, but soldiers stationed much further back than division headquarters received the identical battle stars that we get in the frontlines. These men, who have never had to live with death, obtain the same number of points as the combat infantryman. Does this point system burn us up! Yes, the army seems to look upon the infantry as the scum of the earth. I think it would break their hearts if we ever got a break. Every combat soldier is so furious over the whole deal that one can't talk about the war without mentioning the point system. A soldier needs 85 points or better to even think of being discharged (or go home for that matter). I ended up in the 70s. Don't ask me how.

The military and I never concurred on the number of points I had amassed during my service. I could not argue intelligently with them since there was no way I could retrieve and review my actual records. I had to accept their computations. Their figures were final; take it or leave it. It was not until 2003 that I discovered the error. It was impossible to believe but my discharge and other official records had completely omitted the Anzio campaign (January 22–May 24, 1944). You can imagine how I felt!

May 1945

Dear Folks,

I've been wondering what kind of pictures the media print showing the German concentration camps. Let me tell you those German SS troops have no heart to do some of the atrocities they did. I wish I had some good photographs to show you of the dead, withered, starved bodies and of the truckloads of them. I don't think you could possibly realize what transpired in these camps unless you saw the dead as I did. The SS soldiers did not use stoves for cooking meals but instead put humans in the ovens, and turned on the heat. It wasn't long before one's suffering was over. Sometimes the Germans would pack a room solidly with men, women, and children and leave only a small window open for everyone to use to inhale and exhale. If any child screamed in terror, the SS would close the window and watch the people suffocate. Women took terrible punishment from these "Supermen," but the world has long known this fact. We must never forget the truth.

I see where May 2nd was a day everyone unlimbered their pencils and pens and wrote me. The letters all arrived at the same time along with 3 packages—one from Ruthie, one from Russell, and the other was yours. I read about the sugar cutback; so I won't be expecting as many cookies in the future. That's fine. Hum-m-m! There must be some mistake in your letter. From the latest news communiqué I see that Daddy has cut both the front and back lawns. That couldn't be true, could it? What's he been eating lately? Has he been popping a double dose of vitamin pills? Please tell me the secret, I'm dying to know.

Auntie inquired about my MP job and where I was stationed in the 3rd Division. I am still connected to the 15th Infantry Regiment; the only change is that I do MP work instead of actual frontline combat. I guess we are what you would call combat MPs. Even though the job is safer than actual combat, you could very easily get wounded in wartime.

All My Love,
Bob

Survivors in a Concentration Camp

Change of Routine

May 18, 1945

Dear Folks,

The Army has printed a list of subjects they plan on offering to the G.I.s. We have been told that everyone will be permitted to choose a maximum of four. Subjects range from various languages, history, English, typing, bookkeeping etc. I looked over the list and put a check after journalism, typing, shorthand, and English composition. It will be some time before the Army works out a schedule, but eventually I may pick up a little extra schooling. The Army inquired whether or not we ever taught any subjects or if we were qualified to teach. You see, the teachers will come from our ranks, not professionals. I pondered over elementary mathematics quite a while before deciding to skip teaching. I probably could do the job but the Army undoubtedly wants someone older than I to do the teaching.

I'll zip you another letter in a day or two.

All My Love,
Bob

May 19, 1945

Dear Folks,

I've had so many people tell me what they did on Easter Sunday that I thought I would tell you my story. We were moving by truck through Germany as fast as ever when we reached a small town and decided to stop for a few hours.

As I walked up a narrow street, I saw an old lady in her 70s, crying as she looked at the burnt ruins of her house. There was nothing left but charred timbers. Naturally, she was German. There were no tears of compassion felt for her by any of us. In fact there probably will never be any tears shed for any German man, woman, or child in the immediate future. They and their nation have brought too much misery, pain, and suffering to the world for anyone these days to feel the least bit sorry for them.

Yes, it was Easter Sunday, and you in the States were going to church, out to dinner, or for a walk with your new bonnets. There is something special about Easter. You can feel it in your heart. But to us soldiers who have bitterly fought the Germans tooth and nail these many moons, it was merely another day. The more dead Jerries there were the better. Someday I hope to awaken on Easter morn with a feeling of joy and happiness. I want to feel sorry for those who are not as fortunate as I, but it will take time to heal my wounds. If you had seen the horrible things the Germans did to the French towns, and their citizens or witnessed a concentration camp, then you too would feel like I do. Many friends (especially girls in their teens and early 20s) write and ask how I could stand myself after killing so many German soldiers. They cannot seem to understand this war and what it has done to the people involved. To me the German nation is the blood-thirstiest country in the world. They must pay for their crimes against mankind, or they will return 20 or 30 years hence and begin all over. As sure as I am sitting here today, I am afraid the conquerors will turn soft and not give Germany her just "reward." She must be ruled as a conquered nation, without compassion or sympathy.

Happy Easter,
Bob

P.S. The Easter bunny missed me again this year.

May 26, 1945

Dear Daddy,

Today, I'm going to sit down and write a letter to the fellow from 23 Oakwood Ave. who signs his letters "just daddy, that's all." (Finally, I came to the conclusion that you were the author.)

My discharge-point tabulations seem to read 70 vs. 85 required. The main reason my score is fairly high is because of all my battle stars and Purple Heart. Even though I was "most fortunate" in having the privilege of being in 2 first-wave amphibious assault landings, the point system did not give me any special consideration. Our Division has the most battle stars of any U.S. outfit; ten combat stars; I have 6 such stars which equates to 30 points. The majority of divisions who landed in Normandy have 3 stars. The First and Ninth Divisions also fought in Africa; so they have 4 or 5 battle stars. The Presidential Unit citation carries some weight but the two French Croix de Guerre awards with Palm aren't taken into consideration when computing "points." Our Division has received a record-breaking 431 (or a few more) days of actual frontline combat. I came in at 330–355 days on the front; one of the tops in the regiment. (I owe my life to my guardian angel; make no mistake on that count.) I should be told in another month what will happen to me. I hear the divisions with the highest critical scores will stay in Europe. That should include the 3rd.

With Love to All,
Bob

May 29, 1945

Dear Folks,

We were mighty glad to read in the *Stars and Stripes* that actual combat men will not be sent to the Pacific. Even if our division was scheduled to go, the men who were attached to the Division in Africa, Sicily, and Italy would be transferred out and placed in a unit remaining as Army of Occupation. I had expected it when General Eisenhower first made his statement that African veterans would not go to the Pacific unless they volunteered. I won't go and volunteer for the Pacific. I may have to stay in Europe a little longer, but I will be coming home some day. Next year if they still have 85 as the discharge score, I'll make it easy. At first the top brass said that men who enlisted (as I did) had signed for the duration and would not be included in the point system. However, this week someone woke up and changed the policy so that any soldier who has the required points, providing he is not essential, will be discharged. I am confident no one in the infantry will be classified as essential!

I wrote Russell and let him know where I was located and gave him some pictures of the concentration camps that the SS troops maintained. I understand an average of 200 a day died in these camps. I was told in one camp the Germans had a huge underground room with spikes on the wall. If anyone was considered a trouble-maker, he was brought to this "special" room and spiked to the wall to die. When pronounced dead, his body was carted away to the oven.

No one ever escaped from these closely guarded camps. There was a huge hospital inside the grounds where men who were about to die were assigned. When one's name appeared on the hospital list, he or she knew the end was near. "Scientists" visited these camps regularly and often removed men for experiments. Few, if any, ever returned to the camp alive from these experimental units.

I guess I'd better put Willie's mind at ease by telling him I have some pistols for him. I have a nice Luger and some other real smart-looking weapons. I don't know which ones I'll bring back. Everyone in the rear outfits is trying to get their hands on a German pistol.

With Love to All,
"Two-Gun Pete"

Clean Up Time

May 30, 1945

Dear "23,"

Today, I received my new "dress" jacket and another new shirt to wear. My old one was so torn and dirty that I was ashamed to wear it. Nevertheless, I must admit I hated to part with it. (Sentimental reasons, I suppose.) I have been told that I have to wear a tie whenever I venture away from my Army residence. That's going a mite too far. (I never did like a tie, did I?) I must also wear all my ribbons, battle stars, and French citations. It doesn't stop there either. On top of everything, I have white gloves. (To hide the dirt that is still lodged in my nails.) You would not recognize me anymore. Even my shoes had to shed the mud and look respectable.

"Spic-and-Span,"
Your son,
Bob

June 1, 1945

Dear Willie,

I'm glad you liked the German jacket. I was afraid it would never get home, but I guess no one wanted to "lift" it. I have not sent you a helmet because they are so heavy. I'll try to mail one but don't expect it. I wrapped up some more medals and Jerry flashlights that will be going to you next week. The 2 German iron crosses sell as high as $12 each when I sell them to men in the rear outfits. A Luger pistol brings well over a hundred greenbacks. I will bring mine home instead of using the mail.

Our regiment has to work with all the laborers from other countries that the Germans "imported" into Germany during the war years. The misplaced workers also have to be transported back to their homeland. There are so many faces to feed that the job seems almost impossible. It's lucky the railroads are repaired and working to a degree because they help haul away these people.

With Love to All,
Bob

June 3, 1945

Dear Folks,

I have not been in the MPs three months, and I'm tired already of the job. No excitement. A friend of mine from K company and I are trying to get into another branch of service, namely the signal corps. I don't think either of us will make it, but you never can tell. If I could only get out of the infantry, I'd volunteer to go to the Pacific Theater. However, while I'm still an infantryman, you would not catch me volunteering. I see by our local newspaper that Calvin McLish, a former Brooklyn Dodger pitcher, has joined the 3rd Division and will pitch for us. Our division will play baseball against other divisions; supposedly there will be a playoff to determine the champs of this sector. (Please note I said champs not chumps.)

The True Meaning of "It's Over"

June 6, 1945

Dear Folks,

Daddy sent me some pictures of Times Square the day the war ended in Europe. The people in the buildings must have thrown tons of paper out of the windows. To us it did not seem to mean so much. No soldier shouted in glee; no soldier danced in the streets. We just talked to one another very quietly about our chances of going home or to the Pacific. A few got drunk and passed out. To most of us who had come so far and were so tired and weary, the end of the European phase of the war meant that now we could relax for a while. There would be no more battles to win, no more icy rivers to cross, and we would no longer have to sleep in the rain without any cover or in wet foxholes. We would not have to be on the move continuously, without sleep, and we would not have to eat cold C rations. We would now be able to eat from our mess kit, the food would be warm and appetizing, and showers would be available. We no longer would have to always be on the alert for machine-gun nests, hidden snipers or mines, but instead we could walk across the street unafraid. We wouldn't ever again hear the ugly whine of artillery shells as they dropped close by, nor hear the crack of a rifle and the sing of the bullet as it zipped by your head. But best of all was the fact that we were ALIVE, and there would be no more white crosses added to the thousands already here. Our prayers had been answered. The sound of freedom was everywhere. It was wonderful!

Since I've been writing so much of the war's end, I would like to share with you a little story. It was the day armistice had been declared, and we were moving into Salzburg. Whenever we stopped for a few minutes, some of the fellows would jump out and hunt for eggs. I don't particularly care for eggs, so I had no desire to run around looking for them. Now a chicken, that's a different story. One of my friends thought he would go up the nearby hill and see if there were any eggs in the farm house. He said he'd be back in a minute, and so we didn't pay any further attention to him. Suddenly, there was the crack of a rifle, followed by a deathly silence. No one spoke a word; every eye was turned toward the farmhouse door. Our buddy was seen standing in the doorway, holding on the door for support. Slowly, he turned around and started down the hill, grasping his chest. He did not get more than 10 feet from the building before he collapsed. By the time we reached him he was unconscious. For days he hung on, but one morning we were told the doctor entered his room and found him dead. This fellow had landed with the 3rd Division in Africa, and now on the final day of the European war, a bullet from an SS trooper takes his life. It was so tragic! We tried to find his killer but to no avail.

In the *Stars and Stripes* I read an article from the War Department on the various combat divisions with the greatest casualties. The 3rd Division was hardest hit with 34,224 with the 45th Division second with 27,553.

A year ago today, the Allies landed in Normandy. The Army took time out to remember the sacrifices these brave men made by declaring June 6, 1945 a holiday. We had a day of rest; no guard duty. A full night's sleep was guaranteed. That in itself is a real blessing.

With Love to All,
Bob

I purposely neglected to use the word "sound" but chose "full" because at this stage it was impossible for me to sleep soundly. Nightmares were commonplace.

Military Police

June 7, 1945

Dear Folks,

As I previously mentioned, the military police had an exceptional amount of work to complete trying to get these displaced people back to their own countries. Many Russian women do not want to return home. I guess quite a few will remain in Germany. Most have been here so long that they are looked upon as one of the family and are treated accordingly. In addition, many of their homes in Russia have been destroyed, and their parents and friends killed. As a result they wish to remain where they are in Germany and Austria.

I see you still haven't had any mail from me. Everyone writes and tells us the mail isn't going through; so you are not the only ones awaiting word from overseas.

The main thing I must impress on you is that I will not be home for quite a while. Fortunately, my point score is quite high. Our sergeants say I should be leaving inside 2 months. That translates into "I won't be seeing New York much before Christmas!"

We have to press our clothes regularly. One fellow is a tailor by trade who helps us. I've gotten so that I can press my own clothes pretty good. Surprised? The trousers are the easiest; the shirt is wicked! We are expected to put creases down the front and back of our shirts. That exercise alone takes hours. I don't mind pressing at all, but I hate to do any sewing.

I have to go on guard this afternoon. If the sun is out, I'll take some pictures. I lost the pictures at Salzburg and perhaps the ones at Berchtesgaden. I hated to lose them. My sergeant was going to have them developed. He gave them to the lieutenant (by mistake) and that was the end of the pictures. They disappeared. (The negatives, not the lieutenant.)

With Love to All,
Bob

Berchtesgaden, Austria

June 15, 1945

Dear Folks,

The first thing I must do is tell you a little about these pictures I am sending. Two were taken from a small window in the castle. One shows the winding river that flows directly through the middle of the valley. On either side are huge, snowy mountains. If you look closely, you can see the only bridge for miles around that crosses this swift river. Running parallel to the river is a railroad. When we first arrived here, we had to inspect the railroad cars. Several cars were full of gold! Everywhere you looked there was gold and more gold. The other cars also contained millions of dollars worth of valuables (art paintings, etc.). Additional guards had to be brought in quickly and placed around the area. Eventually, the gold and other valuables were taken by U.S. officials to a safe place, but the story that goes with them still remains.

I took another whole roll of film at a nearby lake known as Emperor's Lake which is outside Berchtesgaden. Hitler used to come here for a little relaxation. It's a simply beautiful spot in the Alps with a boathouse, waterfalls, and motor launches to take you around the lake.

Salzburg is a lovely city with an immense theater. All the major musical shows were produced in this theater in former years.

Bob in Austria

Salzburg, Austria

June 18, 1945

Dear Folks,

A group of us went to Salzburg on Sunday to see the movie *Having a Wonderful Crime*. I didn't care for it, but I seem to have lost interest in movies. My life is changing, and I am having a difficult time adjusting.

We tried to get some doughnuts and ice cream in town but failed; the store was packed. The only trouble with Salzburg is that it is an awful long hitch-hike to get there. You have to cross one mountain range and then follow the river into town. It takes about 2 hours each way, and so I only go once in a blue moon. The last time we went we ate lunch with the signal corps and in the evening with a transportation unit who are desperately searching for new jeep drivers. I could get a job driving anytime I say the word but, personally, I do not want to drive Jeeps in Europe. (Jeeps in the USA would be fine.)

The War Department is about 400,000 men short of their discharge quota. The score of 85 is to be lowered a mite (probably to 80). The problem is the Army is still not shipping anyone home since the war ended. (Except for one early shipment.) They keep claiming a lot will leave soon, but you never can tell. Supposedly, in September, there will be a new tabulation, and by then I'll be over the mark. Nevertheless, I don't think I'll be returning until at least the end of 1945.

I received a postcard of Salzburg from Gene, and I understand he sent one to you. It's a great photo of the city. Unfortunately, you cannot see where we are holed up because we stayed on the outskirts of Salzburg in Himmler's former private home. What a lovely place it was. Hitler, likewise, had a residence in Salzburg. Both homes were full of loot. When the Germans retreated, the citizens swarmed down and removed many works of art for themselves. In fact the hunt still goes on in Salzburg for the "loot."

"Lootless,"
Bob

Battle Credits and Ribbons

June 24, 1945

Dear Folks,

You asked so many questions in regard to the point system that I'd better try to clear the air a mite. In determining battle stars, the military utilizes various dates. Anyone who was in the battle zone during said date was eligible for one star. I have 6 battle stars or one silver service star:

3rd Division—Combat Zone	Period
Naples-Foggia	Nov. 1, 1943–Jan. 21, 1944
Anzio	Jan. 22–May 24, 1944
Rome-Arno	May 25–Aug. 14, 1944
Southern France	Aug. 15–Sept. 14, 1944
Rhineland	Sept. 15, 1944–Mar. 21, 1945
(includes Vosges and Colmar)	
Central Europe	Mar. 22, 1945–May 11, 1945

In addition, I have one arrowhead which signifies a landing made on D-Day. No matter how many landings you participate in, you only wear one arrowhead. My two first-wave amphibious assault landings were Anzio (Jan. 22, 1944) and Southern France—St. Tropez (Aug. 15, 1944).

Under the point system, we receive 5 points per campaign. The Purple Heart adds 5 more. The rest of my points come mainly from time overseas; total 70. There is no question it will take an unbelievably long time to get those being discharged home by ship. All men going to the Pacific via the U.S. leave first. After these troops have been cleared out and their equipment loaded, the men with over 85 points will leave. Of course, the sick and wounded get first call over everyone.

Daddy wrote me a few weeks ago in which he sent me various Army slang words that he found in a magazine article. As far as I am concerned they are all Greek to me. I never heard or used any of them except "Oh, my aching back." This is a very popular saying among the fellows overseas. It generally refers to some tough or undesirable job to perform. In combat, we are always saying it, but the words seem to have been shunted aside now that the war is over. As a rule, you do not find too much Army slang overseas. We probably have 2 or 3 pet sayings and that's all. Believe it or not, we speak English just like the natives in England and Australia.

Speaking of delays, in today's *Stars and Stripes* these was an article stating that our mail has been routed to the states by boat (no mention is made of the type of boat—row boat, sail boat etc.) and have been taking at least 2 weeks longer than usual to get into private mailboxes. For the first time since last March, the mail will henceforth, be flown to the U.S.A. Some 600 plus tons of mail collected these past months in Europe is being unloaded and will soon reach you. (No, they are not all my letters.)

With Love to All,
Ramblin' Bob

June 28, 1945

Dear Readers 'n' Listeners,

I snapped a couple of rolls of film this week and have some more negatives for you. Don't be surprised if you find 4 negatives of some German soldiers in this batch. These pictures were taken by the former owner of the camera before it was liberated by me. You can get an idea of the uniform and equipment the Germans wear. Notice their steel helmets and the pouches around their waist which contain rifle ammunition. When the Krauts are captured, they always throw their helmet away and don woolen caps.

Your Ardent Photographer

A Taste of Heaven

V-Mail—Austria
July 1, 1945

Dear Auntie,

At present I am at a mountain lodge high in the Austrian Alps. From my room I can look down the valley and see numerous tiny farm houses dotting the countryside. About a mile up, the snow begins and a little past the snow lines the clouds came down to hide the rest of the mountain from view. There is not a single thing to do here except eat, sleep, and go mountain-climbing. Four of us tackled the mountain the other day and disappeared into the clouds. We kept laughing, climbing, slipping and sliding in the snow like teenagers. Finally, we reached a gigantic waterfall nestled in the hills. Water gushed down hundreds of feet, straight through the valley. What a sight! Life is wonderful after all.

It seems as though I am reverting to my childhood days. Everything is fine, especially the freedom we are enjoying.

V-mail—Austria
July 4, 1945

Dear "23,"

I'm still here at the rest camp. My three-day rest has doubled itself in time, but I'm not the least bit unhappy. I must admit I have been catching up on sleep. A new group is supposed to drop by tonight; so this should be the end of my rest period. I have to go back and pack anyway because we are moving inside a week.

The food hasn't been too bad. In fact I think the meals are better here than in our company's mess kitchen (or is it messy). We had apple pie one day, but it was not cooked enough. Tonight we are looking forward to more pie. Happy 4th of July. There are no fireworks here, only happy faces.

Bob

July 5, 1945

Dear Folks,

I have just returned from my rest camp on the outskirts of heaven. Today _____ [name censored] is decorating our division for its action in the Colmar Pocket. There is to be a big parade in Salzburg, Austria with the entire division participating. The ceremony was supposed to be held on the Fourth of July but rain prevented it. At eleven o'clock, the _____ of the _____ Army _____ will read the Presidential citation, add the streamer to our division colors, and inspect the troops.

The Presidential citation is the only ribbon worn on the right side of your jacket, over the pocket. We were the first American Infantry division to be so honored. I will be able to wear a cluster to this citation (meaning I have been cited twice by the President) as soon as the 3rd Battalion, of which K company is a part, is officially recognized for their work on Christmas Day. The French citation is worn around the left shoulder and is red and green. The 3rd Division's outstanding role was recognized by the Commanding General of the 1st French Army in February 1945, when he awarded the division its second Croix de Guerre citation.

The fellows with over 85 points were supposed to transfer to another division, but the orders were changed at the last moment. These men are not leaving just yet. Transportation is really bad; it will take much longer to ship the men home than expected. One bright incident did occur; 851 men were flown home on July 2nd. Boy were they a happy, wild bunch of Indians!

With Love to All,
Bob

CHAPTER 12

The Long Awaited Trip Home

Time to Move On

July 15, 1945

Dear Folks,

You probably have surmised I am on the move again since you have not had a letter from me in about a week. We are now at our occupational area in Germany. Our regiment is located 30 miles south of Cassel (The Germans spell it Kassel, but I believe our maps use Cassel.)

July 16, 1945

Dear Folks,

Thank goodness the food in this camp is a hundred percent better than our last "home" base. Our rations are still being reduced, but what the Army dishes out these days in the form of good, wholesome food is at least edible. One day for breakfast I had a small package of cereal such as Grape Nut Flakes, Wheaties, or What-Have-You. I haven't had anything like this since leaving our invasion craft for Southern France. The Navy used to furnish us cereals for breakfast quite regularly. Unfortunately, the Army (or at least our division) was not privileged to such "gourmet" foods.

Incidentally, the British Zone of Occupation is only 18 kilometers from our town—11 1/2 miles approximately. Every once in a while we drop over to visit them. The Australians, who call us the "bloody Yanks," seem to be most like Americans, and we get along great with them. The majority of Australian soldiers are older than we are, but, nevertheless, they think the U.S. military soldiers are tops when it comes to fighting ability. We have seen the Australians in action; they are tough and courageous.

July 18, 1945

Dear Folks,

My pocket watch broke just as I was leaving Werfen, but I'll have a German jeweler take it apart and fix it for me. At present I have a battle-scarred wrist-watch that keeps fairly accurate time. I gave several

German pocket watches to my pals in K company and kept one for myself.

I am not allowed to purchase German products. Every store almost is off-limits to American soldiers except photo and watch shops.

I notice our Rye neighbor, John Wahl, is at Ft. Benning. Boy, he's going to receive some tough training! Major General John W. O'Daniel (our former division commander) is presently in charge of that shop, and he is a mighty rugged fellow. Recruits are bound to receive the best of training under him, but it won't be easy by a long shot. He pushes his men to the utmost. When he gets his division rolling, nothing stops him or the division—the Colmar Pocket was wiped out in 2 weeks, we took Rome 13 days after the Anzio breakout, and we crushed the mighty Siegfried and Maginot fortifications in nothing flat.

It's funny, the war is over, but here I am still in a combat mood. I guess it will take time to calm down and lead a normal life, if my life can ever be described as normal.

With Love to All,
"Battlin' Bob"

Life in General

July 24, 1945

Dear Folks,

I'm moving up in this world. We now have a shower room and can take a hot shower whenever we have time. My pal and I generally drop by the water hole 4 or 5 times a week. Eventually, we should be able to get rid of all the ground-in dirt we still retain from sleeping in foxholes.

I see George Finneran is in a Long Island hospital. It is rough when you are shell-shocked. I mentioned previously how so many soldiers got battle fatigue in the Vosges. You reach a point where your nerves cannot stand it anymore. We had one lieutenant who went to the hospital with battle fatigue on his first day in combat. This happens quite a few times with new recruits who are immediately thrown into combat. It's extremely nerve-racking for anyone to join their new platoon one night and be ready to head out on the attack the very next day. I hope George can recover.

Believe it or not; I received my Tiffany wristwatch back for the last time. It will never be fixed because the jeweler in Paris said the main balance spring is broken. He suggested returning it to Tiffany's and have them repair or replace it. This ends my saga of "The Little Watch That Wouldn't Go."

With Love and a few tears,
Bob

"To the Colors"

July 26, 1945

Dear Folks,

I cannot believe it, but I slipped through yesterday's parade without a mishap! Another first for me. Let me start by saying the ceremony was in front of our regimental headquarters. The flag was raised while the band played "To the Colors." What I did not mention was yours truly was the one chosen for the color guard; I had to hoist the flag. I had never done anything like that before, especially in front of everyone. Photographers were all around the area taking our pictures with the troops in the background. Can you believe it? I didn't miss a beat.

At present we are living in a hotel. The one thing I notice of interest is there are no screens on the windows. In this area there are not too many pesty bugs and mosquitoes waiting to feast on us. You don't have to spend the night swatting your back or listening to that buzz saw dive-bombing your ear. The flies are continually helping themselves to our food. (They must be getting enough to eat 'cuz we certainly aren't.)

All My Love,
Bob

Volunteering

August 1, 1945

Dear Civilians,

I was paid this afternoon, but I am not sending any money home this month. I'll hang on to what little I earn just in case by some miracle I am "elected" to go to a regular rest camp. I can volunteer to go to Switzerland on a 7-day furlough. The only problem is that such a trip is recorded on my service record as a furlough whereas the Army rest camps on the Riviera, Paris, London, and Brussels do not count as furloughs. Very few of the high-point men, yours truly included, want to go to Switzerland because of this regulation plus the fact you are allowed to only spend $35 the entire time you are there—nothing more.

Every man in the U.S. Armed Services is entitled to at least 30 days furlough a year. To date as far as furloughs are concerned, I have a big, fat zero. I doubt if things will improve to any degree before my discharge.

I dropped by the orderly room again this week to get the lowdown on volunteering for the Pacific. After a brief discussion, I realized it was not worth it. I would have to volunteer for an active theater of operations and probably be sent directly to an infantry division in the Pacific. When I and a few of my buddies heard this news, we decided to give up volunteering. I expect I will remain in Germany until I am called to return to the U.S.A. I will not visit my company commander again to arrange for any transfer; so you need not worry about me anymore. Up until yesterday, I had not made up my mind, but I have now.

With Love to All,
"Positive" Bob

Entertainment

August 3, 1945

Dear Willie 'n' Company,

We are beginning to see more current movies nowadays. The last one was *Keep Your Powder Dry* with Lana Turner and Lorraine Day. What a riot! I thought the theater would come tumbling down when Lana Turner was flashed on the screen.

There are a lot of complaints by the troops on how the USO shows are presented. Frank Sinatra wrote the *Stars and Stripes* and admitted the situation was bad. All the big names book their acts only in the major cities. Many soldiers wrote to the newspaper to complain how few soldiers actually receive a chance to see a USO show. This coming Saturday Jack Benny is appearing in Cassel. We can go if we want to make the trip.

Just about every night a couple of my buddies and I drop by the Red Cross for doughnuts and conversation. One evening we even had a surprise glass of Coke. We pay 2 marks (20 cents) for 12 tickets; each drink costs 2 tickets. The doughnuts are free, and you can devour all you want.

Conditions in Europe

August 7, 1945

Dear Civilians,

We are anxiously awaiting word from the President that the war in Japan is over. The radio is on all the time, receiving the latest news flashes. I imagine everyone is doing the same thing all over the world.

I am putting my battle stars in this envelope. I haven't forgotten the division patch for Willie. You'll receive it as soon as I obtain some air-mail envelopes, which will be in 3 days.

For a long time I firmly believed everyone should have a year of military training. However, I have completely changed my mind after I've witnessed how the Army works now that the war is drawing to a close. Just about every soldier is dead set against the military because of the way things are going in Europe. Instead of discharging any men, we are being told that everyone must go to the Pacific, although the brass argue among themselves that the U.S. can't possibly transport these millions of soldiers to the Pacific.

Another major problem with the military is there appears to be no advance planning. We have learned our various military services do not notify the railroads in advance when they will be moving combat troops; so everyone is tossed together in day coaches. You sleep the best you can, if you can.

Here in Europe the food situation is very bad and the entertainment is worse. Presently, we are shown a movie once every 3 days, and it is never a grade "A" movie; only grade "B." The hospitals get the better ones, and they are nothing to rave about. As far as U.S.O. shows, you can grab the paper every day and read some of the difficulties the show encountered. Jack Benny screamed about officials not notifying the troops of his pending presentation. He stressed that he played before 2,000 soldiers in Berlin when the theater held 30,000. No one knew anything about his show, he claimed, until the night he arrived. To make matters worse, Jack Benny had notified the commander 2 weeks in advance. The complaint is the same wherever you look. The military does not seem to care in the least about the men now that combat is over. Oh well, I'll soon be saying goodbye to Europe if Japan falls quickly. See you before year-end.

Love to All,
Bob

The Three R's

August 8, 1945

Dear Folks,

Several moons ago I pointed out that the Army was exploring the possibility of offering several in-house educational courses to soldiers overseas. A lot has been said about this "superb" program, and so I want to keep you abreast and let you know exactly how it works. To start with, several of my friends and I decided to muddy the waters a mite and sign up for some college courses. Before we could sign our names, we were advised that our requests were impossible to fill since all men in regimental headquarters are considered essential! We could attend a regimental school for an hour or so a day. Our own officers (regardless of background) would be the teachers. Only the teachers (commissioned officers) would have textbooks, and it would be up to us, the non-commissioned soldiers, to attend class in our spare time and take notes. Can you visualize how many of us would ever review their notes once the class was finished? In fact how many do you think would bother taking notes, or for that matter, would learn anything worthwhile? The last straw, or should I say ruling, was if an MP attended class, he must do so on his own time. The MP must still pull guard duty. In other words the MP would be working night and day if he wanted any additional schooling. The final result was—one unknown MP signed up for a class.

Another setback was the typing course. It had to be cancelled because there were no typewriters available. I think the most popular course was photography. You had to bring your own camera and film. The Army supplied the locale.

All My Love,
Bob

A Miss Is as Good as a Mile

August 24, 1945

Dear "23,"

Hold tight! Here's some real news. All men with over 75 points will leave our division within 2 weeks and be transferred to a unit slated to head home in September! I just missed the cutoff by one lone point! My 74 points is not quite enough to get me to Rye by September. Hopefully, there will be another shipment in October or November. I'll definitely make that one. I think I should be home to greet good 'ole St. Nick at Christmas. It's been a long road.

There is one thing that I want you to do and that is NOT to send me any Christmas packages this year. There are a million troops going home by year-end, and I definitely should be on the list. I tried to squeeze my 74 points up to 75 points so I could leave with this bunch and be home by September. For some unknown reason, I did not receive any overseas credit for May. If I only had a couple more days to my credit, I would be packing my bags. The officer handling my case tells me my name will head any future "homeward bound" lists; so as soon as the Army locates and counts my May, 1945 days I will be on my way.

We finally received the coveted fourragere to wear with our second French Croix de Guerre citation. It is a red and green cord worn with our jackets. Unfortunately, our division did not receive enough cords for everyone; so only the soldiers who made the Southern France landing received them. Now everyone is happy. I still have to sew on my overseas stripes; but I am such a useless fellow with a needle that I do not know when I'll get the ambition to tackle the job. I only have 4 square inches to sew on my jacket but that is four inches too many.

I have heard a few innings of various Dodger games this year via shortwave. They do not seem to be doing so terrific at this moment. Chickie and her sister, Ann, sent me the latest Dodger paper as well as a letter and a package of socks.

I had a long letter from Daddy in which he inquired about our chaplains. Our chaplain joined our outfit on Anzio and has been with us ever since Italy. All regimental chaplains have the rank of captain (in most cases), while the division chaplain is a lieutenant colonel. Ours is a captain although he joined us as a lieutenant. (At least he got promoted.) He has a Polish name; in fact he has relatives living (hopefully) in Poland. We all love him but without a doubt, he is the worst man alive when it comes to sermons. He just cannot master it.

Nothing else doing; so until next time, I'll say so long.

With Love to All,

Bob

August 25, 1945

Dear Folks,

Here is what has happened so far. The men with 75 points or more (approximately 300 soldiers) are leaving today and joining the 70th Division. Our regiment meantime is accepting as transfers over a thousand men with low points. Bottom line, very soon another bunch of high pointers will ship out, and I'll be one of them. Rumors are flying thick 'n' fast. Some have us pulling out a week from today while others feel it will be a week or two. Whatever the timetable reads, it should not be too long. You must remember that when we leave here, we are shipped to another division that is homeward bound. The 70th is leaving for the states around the middle of September. If we don't join forces with the 70th, we will not be shipping home in September. I doubt if we will hang our helmets in the 70th; so don't expect me back too soon. I will undoubtedly be on the October cruise ship.

With Love to All

August 28, 1945

Dear Folks,

Yesterday, I finally received my Purple Heart, and I didn't have to attend a ceremony to get it. I went to S-1 awards in our regiment and advised them I had never received my medal. They were not going to issue one until I told them I had 74 points and would not be here for the next ceremony. Finally, after much deliberation (and soul-searching) they decided it would be in order to issue the medal without the ceremony. I'll send it home as soon as I find a box.

The *Stars and Stripes* reports that all men with 74 points and over can expect to be civilians by Christmas. I hope it happens! It would be grand to get rid of the O.D.s (olive drab uniforms) and not have to worry about reporting back to camp after Christmas.

I had a beautiful letter from Mrs. Law last evening. She wrote the parents of the lad who was killed in the foxhole with Russell. It seems Russell changed places with him a moment before it happened. What a close call!

With Love to All,
Bob

Arolsen
September 7, 1945

Dear Folks,

It must feel good to be able to pull your car into the gas station and say, "Fill 'er up." How many stations have gone dry because they sold out all their gas?

While on the subject of travel, I must tell you the highways in Germany do not have lights on them. There is not a single super-highway where you will find even a single light pole. Of course, these highways were constructed primarily for the purpose of transporting war supplies and troops. At night the German trucks would drive with blackout lights on, nothing else. If a plane was heard in the immediate vicinity, the trucks would turn off all their lights, and the convoy would hide in the darkness.

These days life is pretty easy compared to the States. All that any serviceman does in Europe is pull guard duty. A little close-order drill is mixed into the menu from time to time. However, I never have to take hikes with full-pack and rifle. When I am not on guard duty, I am free to do what I like. I have had enough hiking from Italy to France to Austria to last me a lifetime. My pack used to tire me out just looking at it, let alone strapping it to my back. One of the problems was that I would always carry an extra blanket to keep me warm in the winter. Top everything off with a machine-gun or ammunition and mud up to your boot tops, and you can understand how difficult it was to maneuver. As I mentioned, many moons ago in France I exchanged my machine gun for a mortar. The weight was about the same—heavy!

With Love to All,
Bob

Pack Your Bags—You Are Going Home

September 13, 1945

Dear Folks,

I finally managed to locate a blank V-mail envelope; so here we go. You should not be writing me anymore because shortly I will be on the move westward and would never receive your communiqués. I understand the trains across the continent are so slow it will take me a few days to get out of the station. I am still in Germany; but by the time this V-mail reaches Rye, I will probably be somewhere along the Northern coast of France.

September 23, 1945

Dear Folks,

I haven't been able to write in over a week; so I'll try to bring you up to date on my progress, if I may be so bold as to call it "progress." I am hanging my shirt 'n' tie in Camp Pittsburg outside of Reims, France. Finally, I have completed my 5-day processing schedule and am fit to return to civilian life. (So the Army tells me.) Now I sit around and "wait for my ship to come in." As soon as one has been salvaged, I will move to a camp outside Le Harve and once again board an ocean-going vessel for an eventual assault on N.Y. In the USA I probably will receive a 30-day furlough and return to camp for discharge.

The officer-in-charge of this camp assures me that once I reach the States, I will "practically be a civilian." (I doubt if I could be ranked a "civilian" in such a short period of time.)

I sold a German gun last month and have a little over a hundred dollars in my wallet, excluding my September pay. That should be plenty to get me to Rye.

The Army has several PXs and movie houses in this camp. The trouble is the camp is so crowded that one has to arrive at the theater at least an hour early to grab a seat. I've skipped just about every movie. In addition, I have a PX card which entitles me each week to 10 packages of cigarettes, 7 candy bars, 2 packs of gum, and whatever else I need. I bought this writing pad since I was out of paper.

With my expertise in the art of hiking, I was pensive the Army would have me walk to Le Harve, France. Fortunately, this was not the case. Seventeen other men and I set out from Lipsenhausen, Germany, on Monday September 17 at eleven o'clock. (Our ticket read First Class.) We were herded aboard a cattle car and told to relax and enjoy the trip.

A wealth of beauty best explains our itinerary, with casual cheer and "untold" luxury. I can truthfully say the service was unexcelled; there was none. Consequently, we did not have to worry about being pampered.

From Monday until midnight Wednesday, we basked in the elegance of our cattle car chugging through Frankfort, Mannheim, across the Rhine River, south toward Metz and concluding in Reims. Once inside France, the Army had regular stopovers where I had hot chow instead of the usual C rations. One point of interest came to light when I was discussing our travel adventures with an Army truck driver. He told me he has taken the same trip many times by truck. A full day was the longest time he ever took to cover this identical area and that included a long stopover in Metz.

We haven't had any mail since leaving the regiment, but we don't have time to worry about the mail. All that we talk about is our boat and when it will arrive. That's it for today.

With Love to All,
"Homeward Bound" Bob

Stop the Press

You never knew what to expect from the Army. And so it came to pass with me and my return to the good 'ole United States. Instead of saying "au revoir" to France and friends from Le Harve, my orders were changed from Northern France to Southern France (Marseille).

October 8, 1945

Dear Folks,

It took me 3 days after leaving Reims to reach my new destination, Marseille. Officially, I am at the Calais Staging area about 10 miles outside the port. I don't do much but pull a little guard. Sailing schedules have been announced as follows:

TYPE OF VESSEL	Anticipated NUMBER OF DAYS
Liberty Ship	15 days
Victory Ship	12 days
Troop Transports	10 days

I hope I don't get stuck on a Liberty ship again. I came over to Casablanca in 21 days in one of them. That was enough for me! My comrades-in-arms and I nearly starved to death on 2 terrible meals a day while the Navy ate the best of food. You would think I was the enemy instead of both services fighting for the same cause. Such is life.

Let's step back a minute and let me tell you about the latest three-day trip from Reims. As usual the train was on the slow to slower schedule. However, I did get a break in that I rode a regular train coach instead of the usual cattle car. What a difference that made! The troops that left Reims after my departure found themselves in cattle cars (minus the cattle). I was lucky in that respect. Our schedule became so mixed up that the train kept missing all the food stops along the way. I had 3 meals the entire trip, but before leaving they gave everyone 3 sandwiches to munch on. By the time the engineer located our final destination, everyone was starving. No one had eaten any food in 14 hours; so we all dove for the mess hall. To give you an idea how slow our train traveled, the last 90 miles took 15 hours. We would go a couple of miles and then sit for an hour or two. What a trip! What progress! Isn't freedom wonderful!

This is my first day in this camp. At Pittsburg each company had its mess hall, but here the whole battalion (700 soldiers) eat in the same place at the same time. What a chow-line there is! It seems endless.

The Krauts do all the KP work. The soldiers returning to the States do not assist with the cooking; the Army has regular mess hall cooks do this work. I know, it's hard to believe our workload is practically nil. So long for now.

Love to All,
Bob

Delays and More Delays

October 14, 1945

Dear Folks,

I have to remain in Europe longer than expected due to a lack of transportation. The transfer of some of the big ocean liners back to England slows the process. In addition, the union strikes in the U.S. ports don't help. The strikes only make us hang around longer in Europe and away from home. It is indeed fortunate the strikers are not in Marseille or Le Harve because they would not last a minute once we Army men got after them. Every member of the armed services is furious over the "strike" situation.

I don't know when I will move out. It does not appear as though I will reach the U.S. much before the middle of November, although I was scheduled to have left several weeks ago.

Every night I go to an open-air movie. It helps pass the time. I have seen *Junior Miss*, *George White's Scandals*, *Out of This World*, and *Don*

Juan Quilligan. Have you seen any of them? Nothing else is new. Don't wait up for me. Leave the light on.

With Love to All,
Bob

My Last Letter from Europe

October 28, 1945

Dear "23,"

Yep, I am still sitting in Marseille doing practically nothing. I have not even been put on the alert list. When I finally read my name on the alert schedule, I will move within 72 hours. (Probably to the next town.) I should not say I do nothing during the daytime. For the last 2 weeks I have been playing volleyball every day. I average 5 or 6 rough, fast games a day. Twice, I have knocked my fingers out of their joints, but after a few days, they come around. With all this continuous playing together, we have turned into an excellent, winning team. Everyone wants to challenge us. One day we played 11 games. That night our legs gave out, and we had to call it quits for a while.

As for evenings, I have not gone to a movie in nearly 2 weeks, but that's because I saw them all at Camp Pittsburg. It's pitch dark by 6:30 p.m.; and since there are no lights in our tents, I generally fall asleep by nine or so. Guard duty beckons me every week. That is a real pain in the neck. I am on duty 4 hours at night and 4 during daytime hours. The problem is we do not need three-quarters of the guards. Unfortunately, our major got mad one day and created numerous extra posts. No other outfit in the camp has as many guards as we do. Some guards are guarding the guards.

At least once a day I walk to the Red Cross to purchase a Coke and a few doughnuts. Do they make a fortune selling Coke! It costs me 4 cents a bottle instead of the usual 5 cents in the States. The Cokes do not taste at all like the ones you buy in the U.S.A., but I buy them to quench my thirst. I have consumed more Cokes this past month than I've put away since leaving the U.S.

I will not get my pay for the month of October until I land in the U.S.; so my bond will not be coming until I draw my monthly $29.55.

Two more ribbons for service troops have been issued—the Victory ribbon and a post-Pearl Harbor one. The Army will distribute them in New York. In due time, there will be an Army of Occupation ribbon too.

I have not been doing much writing recently. Every moment I expect to ship out. Most of us have given up any thoughts of an October sailing; so let's hope I make it in time for a turkey dinner. Can hardly wait to see everyone. It's been too long.

With Love to All,
Bob

Epilogue

Marseille, France:
The Luck of the Draw

Departure: Nov. 3, 1945   Arrival: Nov. 13, 1945

You guessed it! I arrived in Africa aboard a Liberty ship and left Marseille on the same rusty, old "tub." The card games continued where they left off in 1943, and living conditions had not dramatically improved; the transatlantic crossing record would not be broken. However, I did have time to reflect on the past, consider the challenges ahead, and grieve for friends lost forever. No question, we had won; victory was ours; freedom was assured.

The sea seemed more disturbed than usual as we chugged our way out of Marseille, past Gibraltar and out into the vast expanse of the Atlantic Ocean. Next stop, Ft. Dix, New Jersey, our separation center. I could hardly wait to see my family after all these years. And yet. . . .

The Need to Set My Mind at Ease

One morning as I strolled the deck of our Liberty ship, I paused for a moment to review the past few years. Nagging questions that I could not shake flashed through my mind. I later learned that many others fielded similar trepidations. Going home was not quite as easy as it sounded. There would be many rough days ahead. No one could help us. Each of us had to resolve his own particular problem. There was no single, universal correct answer acceptable for everyone.

In general, discussions revolved around what the future held for us. We were returning to a different world than the battle-scarred one we had left. Would we be able to re-adjust and return to a normal life? How long would it take? Where would we fit in? Would the future remember our cause, the cause of freedom, or were our sacrifices all in vain?

Combat soldiers had other deep, troubling questions to address. I could not help but wonder: "Why did I survive while so many of my friends made the ultimate sacrifice?" I was going home, but they would remain on foreign soil for all eternity. As I searched for an answer, I kept recognizing the immense impact the Lord and my guardian angel had on my life. They were always at my side; I never walked alone. They brought me safely through some of the most vicious, bloody, terrifying battles of any war. I cheated death and am here today thanks to their unfaltering efforts.

Fort Dix, NJ

At the convenience of the government, I was given an honorable discharge on November 19, 1945. I retraced my steps to Rye, NY, and started to pick up my life where I left off in 1943.

Return to Civilian Life

Let me start by saying I was no different than the millions of men who served their country in wartime and came home to an uncertain future. At first I was exceedingly apprehensive and unable to discuss the horrors I had endured. However, it was not too long before I could relate to family and friends the many so-called "funny" events that continuously seemed to befall me. Slowly, I began to adjust; the years drifted by. On May 24, 2002 the final bridge was crossed, and I returned with my wife to Anzio and St. Tropez. Memories came rushing back; tears welled up as I stood among the white crosses in the Sicily-Rome cemetery in Nettuno where many of my buddies were laid to rest. In retrospect I came to realize I was not as tough a soldier as I thought I was. Death was much stronger and final.

At the conclusion of the war I accepted the reality that my nerves were shattered. Nightmares were commonplace; loud noises such as a car backfiring or an object falling to the ground often caused a frightening fear to envelop me. I quickly returned to my party days. You could find me at the center of any social event, surrounded by friends. However, do not be misled by my actions. Deep inside, there was a feeling of loneliness; I would walk by myself for hours at a time, reminiscing on those days in Anzio, Colmar, the Vosges Mountains, and other places, where death was my constant companion.

The government was generous to returning veterans. A $20 weekly subsidy for 52 weeks was established for all unemployed "vets." I fit right into the "52–20 club." At night I attended NYU (courtesy of the government) and obtained my college degree. I was happy to be home; slowly my anger subsided.

A housing boom was in the making. Designed communities began to spring up. Home ownership became a possibility for every American for the first time. Carports were born; shuffleboards, bingo, and bowling halls thrived; garages slowly vanished.

From my letters home you could probably ascertain that Ann was my childhood sweetheart and Gene and Russell my close friends. Ann had been such a great gal all those years, writing constantly, sending care packages, and visiting my folks whenever possible. I was indeed the lucky one!

I recognized that my mental wounds sustained in the war would not heal overnight. It would take time. Ann was ready to settle down; I was not. I stepped away and pressed Gene into the matrimonial arena. He commenced dating Ann on a regular basis, and they were happily married a year later. I remained their close friend.

It was not until twelve years after discharge that I finally settled down and married the girl of my dreams, Helen J. Brendel of Rye, NY. We had four fantastic children, Kathleen, Robert Jr., Brian, and Christopher. As the years passed, my wife's health began to deteriorate. She found it harder and harder to maneuver through the day. On June 6, 1975 the angels came and took her from us. Thanks to my wonderful children, I survived once again.

Lady Luck was still with me in 1987 when I joined forces with an old friend, Bobbe Rice of Manhasset, NY. With her six children, my four, plus grandchildren, we married and set out to conquer the world. Happiness abounded; life was beautiful!

Postscript

On April 10, 1945 as World War II was drawing to a close, I decided I would condense my war experiences into a book to be entitled *A Letter Marked Free*. The initial introduction and first chapter were forwarded to my parents to be held for my return. The savageness of the war and the scars of battle were fresh in my mind. I could still vividly see the bodies of my buddies being ripped apart, the screams of terror, and the cries for "medic."

Unfortunately, I was never able mentally to take up my pen and write my war story until my son, Brian, started to hound me in early 2005. "Future generations need to have an insight into the utmost feelings of a combat soldier as he readies himself for the ultimate sacrifice," he said. And so my old war memories, stored away in the corner of my mind, were rekindled. The dust from my letters home was removed. *A Letter Marked Free* was reborn.

In general, anyone in the military service during wartime recognizes early in his career that he will never be returning home (unless wounded or disabled) until the enemy has capitulated. There is a job to be done with no strings attached. In WWII we were proud to serve our nation, seldom thinking of the dangers. The sacrifices were far greater than one ever imagined, but the final result made it worthwhile. Freedom is an expensive commodity; it can never come without a price tag.

The *New World Dictionary of the American Language* describes a hero as "any man admired for his courage, nobility or exploits." I cannot emphasize strongly enough that anyone who volunteered or was drafted into the military is a real hero. You can be proud of each and every one of them. Stand up and salute them for they are the greatest!

As any WWII veteran will relate, it takes less than a moment to breach the bridge between life and death. There were many occasions whereby I stood in the shadow of the bridge, ready to cross over. I never took that final step. However, four hundred seven thousand Americans did cross the bridge for the cause of freedom.

With Love to All,
Bob

A Letter Marked Free
AS IN FREEDOM

GOD BLESS AMERICA

Appendix

List of Players

Bob's Family—Auntie, Billy, Mom, Dad

Family

Mom or Mimi: mother, Ethel A. Lynch, homemaker

Dad or Daddy: father, William F. Lynch, banker

Billy or Willie or Frenchie: younger brother, William G. Lynch. Attended Milton, Rye High School, and NYU. Willie became a corporate executive and married Gloria Henry of Rye. They have two children and two grandchildren.

Auntie: maternal aunt, Elizabeth Baker Armstrong, elementary school teacher in Yonkers, NY

Ruthie: maternal aunt, Ruth Gilchrist, lived on Long Island, NY

Chickie & Ann Mulvey: cousins, daughters of Dearie and Jim Mulvey. Their grandmother, Tessie McKeever, was my father's sister.

"23": 23 Oakwood Ave., parents' residence in Rye, NY

Friends

Ann Reilly: my high school sweetheart; she married Gene White.

Gene White: long-time friend, neighbor, and Rye High School schoolmate; attended Fordham University. Gene married Ann Reilly; they have four children and six grandchildren.

Jean Wilson: long-time friend of parents, former secretary of NY Giants Baseball Club

Mary Stuart: close friend of Aunt Elizabeth Armstrong, teacher in Yonkers, NY

Russell S. Law: war-time friend and hero, wounded in Anzio. Russell married his high school sweetheart, Mildred B. Branson, in 1946. They have six children, seven grandchildren, and five great grandchildren.

Other

Guardian Angel: my constant companion and savior. Everyone is blessed with having a guardian angel who acts as our guide and protector. Mine is one of the greatest! He is one tough angel.

Poem Bob Carried in War

"What Did You Do Today, My Friend?"

"What did you do today, my friend,
From morning until night?
How many times did you complain
The rationing is too tight?
When are you going to start to do
All the things you say?
A soldier would like to know, my friend,
What did you do today?

"My gunner died in my arms—
I feel his warm blood yet;
Your neighbor's dying boy gave out
A scream I can't forget.
On my right a tank was hit,
A flash and then a fire,
The stench of burning flesh
Still rises from the pyre.

"He met the enemy today
And took the town by storm.
Happy reading it will make
For you tomorrow morn.
You'll read with satisfaction
The brief communique
We fought but are you fighting?
What did you do today?

"What did you do today, my friend,
To help us with the task;
Did you work harder and longer for less,
Or is that too much to ask?
What right have I to ask this,
You probably will say,
Maybe, now, you'll understand,
YOU SEE, I DIED TODAY."

Poem Bob Carried with Him During WWII

"What Did You Do Today, My Friend?"

What did you do today, my friend,
    From morning until night?
How many times did you complain
    The rationing is too tight?
When are you going to start to do
    All the things you say?
A soldier would like to know, my friend,
    What did you do today?

My gunner died in my arms—
    I feel his warm blood yet;
Your neighbor's dying boy gave out
    A scream I can't forget.
On my right a tank was hit,
    A flash and then a fire,
The stench of burning flesh
    Still rises from the pyre.

He met the enemy today
    And took the town by storm.
Happy reading it will make
    For you tomorrow morn.
You'll read with satisfaction
    The brief communiqué
We fought but are you fighting?
    What did you do today?

What did you do today, my friend?
    To help us with the task;
Did you work harder and longer for less,
    Or is that too much to ask?
What right have I to ask this,
    You probably will say,
Maybe, now, you'll understand,
    YOU SEE, I DIED TODAY.

3rd Infantry Division Casualties

Campaign Dates	KIA	WIA	MIA	Total Battle Casualties	Non-Battle Casualties
Southern Italy Sept. 14, 1943 to Jan. 21, 1944	683	2,412	170	3,265	12,959
Anzio Beachhead Jan. 22, 1944 to May 22, 1944	1,074	4,302	919	6,295	6,455
Breakthrough to Rome May 23, 1944 to June 14, 1944	511	2,575	235	3,321	6,783
Southern France Aug. 15, 1944 to Sept. 14, 1944	218	1,072	401	1,691	1,583
Vosges Mountains/ Early Colmar Sept. 15, 1944 to Jan. 21, 1945	1,277	4,852	108	6,237	7,895
Colmar Pocket Jan. 22, 1945 to Mar. 14, 1945	317	1,410	323	2,050	2,550
Germany/Austria Mar. 15, 1945 to May 8, 1945	373	1,744	416	2,533	1,909
Totals	**4,453**	**18,367**	**2,572**	**25,392**	**40,134**

These figures were provided by the AC or S, G-1, 3rd Infantry Division. North Africa and Sicily campaigns not included.

Over 400,000 Americans died in WWII. It has been estimated that between 50 and 55 million people died in total in WWII.

Overseas American Military Cemeteries

In March 1923 by an act of Congress, the American Battle Monuments Commission was born. They have the responsibility of designing and maintaining in foreign countries the final internment of the remains of American military dead. Fourteen such permanent cemetery sites were established in foreign countries after WWII. Each grave is marked with a white marble headstone: a Star of David for those of Jewish faith and a Latin cross for others. The deceased name, rank, service, organization, date of death, and state from which he entered the military service appears on each headstone. These cemeteries are open 365 days of the year. The American Battle monuments Commission will provide, upon request and without cost, general and specific information concerning the cemetery and exact burial site of the decedent. The address of the ABMC is:

American Battle Monuments Commission
Court House Plaza, Suite 500
2300 Clarendon Blvd.
Arlington, VA 22201

www.abmc.gov

French Legion of Honor

On January 22, 2007 by a decree signed by the President of the French Republic, the prestigious French Legion of Honor medal was bestowed upon the author as "an expression of gratitude and appreciation from the French people for (his) decisive role in the liberation of France during World War II."

This medal is France's highest civilian and military award. An official ceremony took place aboard the French frigate *Primauguet* in the Port of Miami on July 24, 2007.

The Legion d' Honneur is a French order established by Napoleon Bonaparte on May 19, 1802. "It is the premier order of France and its award is, therefore, considered a great distinction. The order is conferred upon men and women, either French citizens or foreigners, for outstanding achievements in military and/or civil life. Maximum quotas for each class have been established." The President of France is the grand master of the order and appoints all other members of the order, by convention, on the advice of the government.

Bob and His Family at the Legion of Honor Ceremony

Samples of V-mail and Cartoons

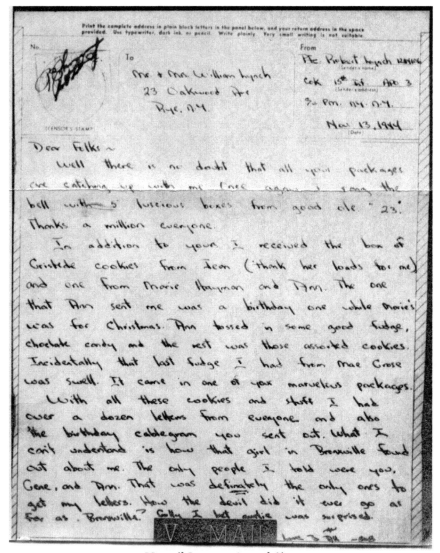

V-mail Letter – Actual Size

V-mail was an efficient method of sending mail from the front. Service personnel wrote a letter on special V-mail paper, which was transferred to microfiche and sent to the U.S. where it was then printed on 4 x 5 paper and mailed to the recipient.

War Humor

The Bells of Vesoul—The Bells of Freedom

Vesoul, France, is an extremely important segment in my life for it is here I discovered, many years later, the real meaning of True Love. The bells of Vesoul are a symbol of this love.

Let me start by saying I was privileged to have had a vital roll in this narrative, which began early on September 12, 1944. Elements of the 3rd Battalion, 15th Regiment of the 3rd Infantry Division had fought their way through strong enemy resistance to the outskirts of their next objective—VESOUL.

As K Company started to enter the city, our scouts walked directly into a machine-gun nest. The events that followed were recorded in my letter home:

> Before we knew it, several of our boys were killed. The French brought their bodies to the entrance of the village, folded their hands over their chests and covered their bodies with flowers. All during the day people would go to church, bow their heads in silent prayer, and walk slowly away with tears running down their cheeks. These people were so heart-broken over the death of these unknown soldiers that sacrificed their lives for them that they would do anything to try to please us. The mayor told us that the people of Vesoul would never forget this morning when they saw the Americans marching over the hill towards their town.

By mid-afternoon Vesoul had been liberated. The bells of Vesoul began to tell their message of freedom throughout the countryside.

In time my memory of these events slipped into oblivion. However, while writing my memoirs, fate stepped in. You can imagine my astonishment when I commenced searching for war pictures and ran across an article concerning Vesoul's dedication on September 12, 2006 of a plaque in memory of the soldiers of the 3rd Infantry Division. The words uttered in 1944 by the mayor of Vesoul hit me like a bomb! Vesoul never forgot! Each year at 2 p.m. on September 12th, the bells toll their message of love to the world as their citizens gather in the city square to pay homage.

Various contacts with the mayor of Vesoul were undertaken in early 2007. The complete story was picked up by several Florida, USA newspapers during my Legion of Honor ceremony on July 24, 2007 in Miami aboard the French destroyer *Primauguet*.

Plaque in Vesoul Dedicated to 3rd Infantry Division

Since the beginning of time we have been taught that the three most important words known to mankind are "I Love You." Today, it is time to add three more to our vocabulary—"We Never Forgot."

O Lord, Unto Your Hands
I Return the Soul of This
Hero Who Fought So Gallantly
for the Cause of Freedom

Priest Giving Last Rights to Fallen Soldier

CPSIA information can be obtained at www.ICGtesting.com
Printed in the USA
LVOW06s0157120913

352033LV00001B/4/P